EDUCATING FOR CRITICAL DEMOCRATIC LITERACY

Educating for Critical Democratic Literacy educates pre and in-service elementary school teachers in teaching four key civics concepts through social studies and literacy integration. Written together by both literacy and social studies experts, it is based on a conceptual revision of the notions of civic education and critical literacy called "Critical Democratic Literacy" (CDL). The authors' dual expertise allows them to effectively detail the applications of their knowledge for teachers, from lesson conception to implementation to assessment.

Part I explains the theory and basic principles of CDL and provides background information on the role of democracy in education. Part II consists of four sample lessons designed using the National Council for the Social Studies (NCSS) C3 Framework and the Common Core State Standards for English/Language Arts (CCSS ELA) standards. Part III includes a primer explaining the four civic concepts that frame the book. Fully aligned to both the CCSS ELA and NCSS C3 Framework, this timely resource provides future and current teachers with specific lessons and tools, as well as the skills to develop their own rigorous, integrated units of study.

Kathryn M. Obenchain is an associate professor in the Department of Curriculum & Instruction at Purdue University.

Julie L. Pennington is an associate professor of Literacy Studies at the University of Nevada, Reno.

EDUCATING FOR CRITICAL DEMOCRATIC LITERACY

Integrating Social Studies and Literacy in the Elementary Classroom

Kathryn M. Obenchain and Julie L. Pennington

NEW YORK AND LONDON

First published 2015
by Routledge
711 Third Avenue, New York, NY 10017

and by Routledge
2 Park Square, Milton Park, Abingdon, Oxon, OX14 4RN

Routledge is an imprint of the Taylor & Francis Group, an informa business

© 2015 Taylor & Francis

The right of Kathryn M. Obenchain and Julie L. Pennington to be identified as authors of this work has been asserted by them in accordance with sections 77 and 78 of the Copyright, Designs and Patents Act 1988.

All rights reserved. No part of this book may be reprinted or reproduced or utilised in any form or by any electronic, mechanical, or other means, now known or hereafter invented, including photocopying and recording, or in any information storage or retrieval system, without permission in writing from the publishers.

Trademark notice: Product or corporate names may be trademarks or registered trademarks, and are used only for identification and explanation without intent to infringe.

Library of Congress Cataloging in Publication Data
Obenchain, Kathryn M., author.
 Educating for critical democratic literacy: integrating social studies and literacy in the elementary classroom / By Kathryn M. Obenchain and Julie L. Pennington. — 1st published 2015.
     pages cm
 Includes bibliographical references and index.
 1. Critical pedagogy—United States. 2. Civics—Study and teaching (Elementary)—United States. I. Pennington, Julie L., author. II. Title.
 LC196.5.U6O25 2015
 370.11′5—dc23
                    2014041095

ISBN: 978-1-138-81374-8 (hbk)
ISBN: 978-1-138-81375-5 (pbk)
ISBN: 978-1-315-74790-3 (ebk)

Typeset in Bembo
by diacriTech

Printed and bound in the United States of America by Publishers Graphics, LLC on sustainably sourced paper.

We dedicate this book to all of the teachers dedicated to helping their students become virtuous, resilient, and engaged members of the democratic community. We applaud their continued commitment to their students and to their own learning, while working under the unrelenting pressures of accountability and high-stakes testing.

K. M. O. and J. L. P.

I dedicate this book to the memory of my parents who taught me to love and respect the discipline of history. To my father, a World War II veteran, who inspired my love of country; and to my mother, an independent and brilliant woman born a generation too early, who inspired me to push against the boundaries and expectations set by others. Together they also taught me the importance of serving the greater good. I thank them both.

K. M. O.

I dedicate this book to my father, who taught me to not only seek to understand history, but to continually question it; and to my mother, who taught me the resiliency and tenacity to do both.

J. L. P.

CONTENTS

Illustrations	ix
Preface	xi
Acknowledgements	xvii

PART I
Understanding Critical Democratic Literacy　　　**1**

1　Educating for Critical Democratic Literacy　　　3

2　Critical Democratic Literacy: Fostering Informed Resilient Engagement in a Democratic Society　　　16

PART II
Teaching Critical Democratic Literacy　　　**31**

3　What Can I Do to Be a Good Citizen? A Kindergarten Unit on Civic Virtue　　　33

4　When and How Should I Get Involved in Civic Life? A Third-Grade Unit on Civic Engagement　　　56

5　How Should I Talk About Important Civic Issues? A Fourth-Grade Unit on Civil Discourse　　　81

6 What Can I Do When a Law Is Unjust? A Fifth-Grade
   Unit on Civil Disobedience   105

PART III
Implementing Critical Democratic Literacy   127

7 Critical Democratic Literacy: Key Concepts and Pedagogy   129

8 Critical Democratic Literacy: Resources for Application
   and Implementation   143

Index   154

ILLUSTRATIONS

Figures

Figure 3.1 Malala's decision	51
Figure 3.2 Amy's decision to share her markers using the criteria of civic virtue	52
Figure 4.1 Primary source analysis: Votes for women	69
Figure 4.2 What does it mean to be "on task"?	74
Figure 4.3 Civic engagement blank concept web	75
Figure 4.4 Civic engagement concept web	76
Figure 4.5 Claiming the right to vote timeline	76
Figure 8.1 Sequencing in search of patterns	144
Figure 8.2 Primary source comprehension	145
Figure 8.3 Inquiry literacy	146
Figure 8.4 Historical readers' theater	147

Tables

Table 3.1 Process guide for planning a unit on civic virtue	37
Table 3.2 The most important thing	41
Table 3.3 The most important thing: Focus on a person	43
Table 3.4 Learning objectives	45
Table 3.5 The most important thing: Focus on a person	48
Table 3.6 Heroes and heroines of civic virtue	49

Table 4.1	Process guide for planning a unit on civic engagement	60
Table 4.2	Learning objectives	71
Table 4.3	Biography timeline questions	73
Table 5.1	Process guide for planning a unit on civil discourse	86
Table 5.2	Civil discourse T-Chart	92
Table 5.3	Learning objectives	93
Table 5.4	Revised civil discourse T-Chart	97
Table 5.5	James Madison and the Bill of Rights inquiry	99
Table 5.6	Cell phone hypothesis template	100
Table 5.7	Cell phone hypothesis graphic organizer	101
Table 6.1	Process guide for planning a unit on civil disobedience	108
Table 6.2	Learning objectives	115
Table 6.3	Civil disobedience definition	120
Table 6.4	Civil disobedience definition (revised)	121
Table 6.5	Selma to Montgomery March at Edmund Pettus Bridge	122
Table 6.6	Protests in Ukraine	123
Table 7.1	Civic virtue across the elementary grades: Additional ideas for lessons on civic virtue	131
Table 7.2	Civic engagement across the elementary grades: Additional ideas for lessons on civic engagement	134
Table 7.3	Civil discourse across the elementary grades: Additional ideas for lessons on civil discourse	135
Table 7.4	Civil disobedience across the elementary grades: Additional ideas for lessons on civil disobedience	138
Table 7.5	NCSS and IRA standards	140
Table 8.1	Content knowledge planning	149
Table 8.2	Pedagogical content knowledge planning	150
Table 8.3	Curricular knowledge planning	150
Table 8.4	Strategic knowledge planning	151
Table 8.5	Instructional process planning guide	151

PREFACE

Our children should learn the general framework of their government and then they should know where they come in contact with the government, where it touches their daily lives and where their influence is exerted on the government. It must not be a distant thing, someone else's business, but they must see how every cog in the wheel of a democracy is important and bears its share of responsibility for the smooth running of the entire machine.

Eleanor Roosevelt

Educating young citizens by bringing Critical Democratic Literacy (CDL) to K–5 classrooms is crucial to the advancement of our democracy. This book has been in our minds and in our teaching since, at least, 2007. By that time, we had been colleagues at the University of Nevada, Reno (UNR) for more than five years, with offices across the hall from one another. Over conversations in that hallway and sometimes on the nearby ski slopes of Lake Tahoe, we (Kathy, a social studies teacher educator, and Julie, a literacy teacher educator) talked about our hopes and frustrations with education. We shared the belief that education, becoming learned, is the way to make life better for oneself and for one's community. Becoming educated is the way for our democracy (i.e., republic), to not just survive, but to thrive, grow, and change with the increasing complexity of our nation and world. We both also believed that working toward this goal was consistently derailed in schools.

Kathy, a college history major, former social studies teacher, and now a social studies teacher educator, witnessed the growing absence of social studies (including the disciplines of civics, economics, geography, and history) in elementary classrooms. For me, long inspired by philosopher John Dewey, as well as the citizenship education purpose of social studies, I became increasingly frustrated by the lack of social studies, and increasingly interested in figuring out what I could do to get social studies back in the elementary classroom. The federal No Child Left Behind (NCLB) legislation of 2001 intended to make sure that all students received a quality education with high quality teachers, included high-stakes accountability measures and the narrowing of the curriculum (what gets taught) and narrowing of instructional practices (how it is taught). NCLB was interested in students' math and language arts scores and, in many elementary schools, these two subject areas became the sole focus of the school day as schools were understandably fearful of the punitive aspects of NCLB. NCLB was followed by the Race to the Top (RTT) federal legislation of 2009 that further intensified the math and language arts focus and the punitive aspects of testing. This was the environment that I was sending my elementary education preservice teachers into. Many of these preservice teachers were already cautious and even uninterested in teaching social studies. Many had uninspired memories of social studies, remembering the chore of reading out of the textbook and answering questions at the end of each section. These memories, combined with the classroom observations that were part of their teacher education program, in which they rarely saw social studies being taught, created more frustration. Of course, there were always a few memories of exciting simulations and field trips, and the gem of being assigned to observe a teacher who had a passion for social studies and the resilience to weather the accountability pressures. These teachers relied on their professional knowledge, continued to be learners as they navigated accountability pressures, and continued to teach powerful and purposeful social studies. They were rare.

Julie, an elementary reading teacher, and now a literacy teacher educator, experienced the narrowing of literacy instruction from both perspectives. I taught before high-stakes testing, and in my first year of teaching I was required to integrate my content area instruction within my literacy teaching by relying on state standards and research. There was no set program and I was not required to use any basal series or textbooks; I collected and created my own materials based on my students' progress. My school community was engaged civically in the larger school district and advocated on behalf of the students often. As teachers we worked with parents and spoke before the school board and wrote letters in support of structures and programs for our students. After a decade of creating a school community with a shared governance model where teachers and parents designed curriculum that created a dual language program, a multi-age grade configuration, and opened up literacy instruction, we were subjected to a high-stakes testing model. The high-stakes testing requirements altered the school and my instruction irrevocably. The dual language program ceased, we were required to use particular scripted programs, and we were evaluated based on how our students scored on the tests (Pennington, 2004). As a teacher, I still worked to integrate my literacy instruction with my social studies and science lessons, but the reading program was set on a skills-based model and my teaching was monitored for program fidelity. After leaving the classroom and moving to teacher education in 2002, history repeated itself as NCLB stretched across the country. Teachers in my courses began describing their teaching in ways quite similar to my own experiences. Some felt tied to the new requirements, while others sought ways to maintain their autonomy. Teacher education became a way for me to assist teachers in understanding not only literacy, but also how to remain educated and resilient in the context of policy-driven instructional mandates.

These experiences and backgrounds were part of our conversations about what we could do differently and perhaps how we might find a way to build on our common interests—fostering the education of resilient, informed, and engaged democratic citizens. We began to focus on integrating social studies and literacy as one way to bring social studies back into the elementary classroom and to move literacy education beyond a functional literacy approach. Working within a traditional teacher education program in a traditional university in which collaboration and, particularly, co-teaching did not fit into teaching load requirements, we looked for other opportunities. One semester, Julie sat in on Kathy's social studies methods course with a goal of providing a literacy voice and perspective to social studies. It was informative for both of us, but not enough. During this time, we also took the opportunity to work with a local school district conceptualizing a new grant for the federally funded *Teaching American History* grant program. The new grant focused specifically on creating teacher professional development centered on the integration of literacy and history in the elementary grades. Developing and teaching these professional development courses provided us with the space to further conceptualize the idea of CDL, how it could become part of the elementary classroom, and the role of integrating literacy and social studies. We worked with teachers representing all of the elementary grades, helping them to develop and then teach lessons that used the social studies and literacy curricula to support their students' growth as citizens. We all worked on better understanding the nuances of integration and the need to honor each of the disciplines being integrated by teaching and assessing important content and skills.

We have also co-developed and co-taught a graduate course that is part of UNR's online Literacy Studies master's program. This provides another space for us to work with teachers and to continue developing the philosophy and practices of CDL. We work with some talented teachers who have taken CDL into their own classrooms. This includes first-grade teacher, Michelle Findley, who you will meet in Chapter 2. This book is one more space for our work in CDL. It represents our current conceptualization of CDL and why we believe it is important. We also believe that what we have included in the book will help teachers incorporate CDL, while continuing to work under numerous constraints.

Purpose and Organization of the Book

The purpose of this book is to educate elementary teachers and students in CDL using social studies and literacy integration. In particular, we focus exclusively on the social studies content areas of history and civics. The book is designed for both preservice teachers and practicing teachers who are interested in teaching their students civic concepts in meaningful ways. The book includes eight chapters that are organized into three distinct parts.

Part I: Understanding Critical Democratic Literacy

Part I of the book consists of Chapters 1 and 2 and provides you with a foundational understanding of democracy, social studies and civic education, and critical literacy. In addition, it explains the theory and basic principles of CDL, providing background information on the role of democracy in education and gives an example of a teacher who has applied CDL in her first-grade classroom. In particular, Chapter 1 details the need for CDL in today's elementary schools, while Chapter 2 explains the theoretical and philosophical framework that supports CDL and demonstrates its application to elementary education. We know that CDL is an unfamiliar term comprising familiar terms, and we spend substantial time in Part I building a case for CDL, as well as defining it.

Part II: Teaching Critical Democratic Literacy

Part II of the book includes Chapters 3–6, with each chapter providing a detailed, multi-part and integrated social studies and literacy lesson on one of four key civic concepts related to CDL. Chapter 3 details a kindergarten series of lessons that teach the concept of civic virtue. Chapter 4 details a series of lessons for third graders on the concept of civic engagement. Civil discourse is the key civic concept in Chapter 5, which includes a detailed series of lessons for fourth graders. Finally, Chapter 6 focuses on the civic concept of civil disobedience, as taught through a series of lessons in fifth grade. In each of these four chapters, the detailed lessons demonstrate how teachers plan, implement, and assess their students, using a variety of social studies and literacy instructional strategies. Each chapter begins by providing some social studies content, particularly historical content. The content overview, while not exhaustive, will get you started on thinking about the social studies content that is necessary to plan and teach the lessons. Just as Part I of this book provides an orientation to CDL, but includes more information than you would take into your classroom, the content knowledge at the beginning of each of the lesson chapters is in addition to the content that the students will learn. This is deliberate. As teachers, we need *plus-knowledge*. That is, we need to know more than we will teach: (1) to understand the larger societal and educational goals, (2) to understand what content must be included and what is optional in order to help students learn, (3) to know how to organize content learning, and (4) to know what to include. We must know more about the topic than just what the textbook or children's literature sources include. You will also notice sidebars in each of these chapters. They call attention to the ways the lessons, be it topic or instructional strategy, address the goal of fostering CDL. All of the lessons are designed using the National Council for the Social Studies C3 Framework (National Council for the Social Studies [NCSS], 2013) and the Common Core State Standards for English/Language Arts (National Governors Association Center for Best Practices & Council of Chief State School Officers [NGA & CSSO], 2010). We recognize that these standards may or may not be appropriate for your particular context, but we wanted to model the use of standards to guide the development of learning objectives and assessment, as well as the choice of appropriate instructional methods.

Part III: Implementing Critical Democratic Literacy

Part III of the book includes Chapters 7 and 8. These two chapters end the book by focusing on every teacher's desire to add to their knowledge base. Implementing CDL in your classroom requires thoughtful planning and preparation. Chapter 7 defines key concepts and principles related to CDL, including key instructional strategies. Chapter 8 contains several planning guides to assist you in designing lessons for your own classroom beyond the sample lessons provided in Part II. We have used these planning guides in our professional development work. The teachers we worked with have found these helpful, not just with CDL lessons, but also with their integrative planning in general.

We hope you enjoy, are challenged by, and learn new ideas through your interaction with our book. In writing this book, we have enjoyed, been challenged, and learned a great deal. We would love to hear your thoughts and ideas about CDL and integrating social studies and literacy in your own classrooms.

References

National Council for the Social Studies. (2013). *Social studies for the next generation: Purposes, practices, and implications of the college, career, and civic life (C3) framework for social studies state standards.* Silver Spring, MD: Author.

National Governors Association Center for Best Practices & Council of Chief State School Officers (NGA & CSSO). (2010). *Common Core State Standards for English Language Arts and literacy in history/social studies, science, and technical subjects.* Washington, DC: Authors. Retrieved from http://corestandards.org/ELA-Literacy/.

Pennington, J. L. (2004). *The colonization of literacy education: A story of reading in one elementary school.* New York, NY: Peter Lang.

ACKNOWLEDGEMENTS

We wish to thank Sue Davis, the grant director for the *Teaching American History* grants in Reno, Nevada. The professional development work we did for the grant was our first laboratory and supported our early forays into the integration of social studies and literacy. We also thank Michelle Findley, an extraordinary teacher, who continues to share her insights and her classroom practices with us. UNR graduate student Hannah Carter tracked down numerous photo sources for us and kept us organized. We thank her for all of her work.

At Routledge, we wish to thank our editor, Catherine Bernard, for her guidance and support throughout the writing of this book.

PART I
Understanding Critical Democratic Literacy

1
EDUCATING FOR CRITICAL DEMOCRATIC LITERACY

> *I know of no safe depository of the ultimate powers of the society but the people themselves; and if we think them not enlightened enough to exercise their control with a wholesome discretion, the remedy is not to take it from them but to inform their discretion.*
>
> Thomas Jefferson

As Jefferson laid the foundation for a democratic society (or more accurately a democratic republic or representative democracy), he understood the necessity of empowering its people and that a democracy required informed citizens. Galston (2001) explains that "democracies require democratic citizens, whose specific knowledge, competences, and character would not be as well suited to nondemocratic politics" (p. 217). Therefore, one of the long-standing purposes of education, particularly public education, is the education of citizens, or as Jefferson stated, "the people themselves."

The United States is built upon political philosophies detailed within the founding documents that clearly delineate what is required of its citizens, beginning with the Declaration of Independence's statement that governments need the "consent of the governed" in order to exist. Collectively, we, as citizens, are the "governed" and it is in our individual and collective best interests to make sure that we are well informed so that the advice and consent we provide is thoughtful, informed, and supportive of democratic ideals. Our role as citizens is reinforced in the Preamble to the US Constitution as it begins with "we the people" and not "we the states." Privileging the people over the states was a deliberate decision made by the framers to strengthen the role of the individual citizen in political and civic life. For example, the House of Representatives, as defined in the Constitution, is the people's house. Its members represent the people of the United States, not the states. While we may elect representatives in our republican form of government, those representatives must be chosen by informed voters wisely and they must continue to be thoughtfully advised of the decisions that they should make to benefit the people of the nation, the nation itself, and in world affairs.

To fulfill the call of our founding documents, we need to be informed about our political institutions, their responsibilities, and their limits. We should understand key ideas, including how the idea of separation of powers differs from the idea of a balance of powers. We should know what our political and human rights are and we should possess the dispositions to value those rights and retain the skills needed to protect them for ourselves and others. As important as it is to be informed, we also need to knowledgeably and skillfully participate in political and civic life. The ability to productively engage in civic life is not innate. It has to be taught. We need to learn how to do this, and we need to help our students learn what is necessary for their participation. Educating citizens is an immense and worthy task. Our purpose as teachers is to educate citizens with all that they need to fulfill this most important role. According to Ichilov (2011), we should educate citizens in order to liberate and empower them to live their lives fully through a strong civic life. One way we can do this is through the disciplines of social studies and literacy.

Civic Education and Social Studies

Civic or citizenship education focuses on the content knowledge, democratic skills, and democratic dispositions required by educated citizens. Civic education can be a part of the formal curriculum in any academic discipline, as well as the informal curriculum. Examples in the informal curriculum include experiences like student council, classroom rules, playground policies, and service projects. However, civic education is most often found as part of the social studies curriculum. Social studies is often defined as the integrated study of the social sciences and humanities for the purpose of civic competence (Engle & Ochoa, 1988). There are three key components to this definition. First, social studies includes integration. For example, it is difficult to teach a really important event in history, like Westward Expansion, and just focus on history. The geographic themes of movement, place, and human-environment interactions; economic concepts that examine patterns and varied types of economic activity; political science ideas related to power and governance; and even the critical challenges to the term Manifest Destiny, all contribute to a deeper examination and understanding of this period in history. The second component in the definition of social studies is the reliance on the social sciences and humanities. As illustrated in the Westward Expansion example, social studies includes a variety of social science disciplines, including economics, geography, history, and political science, as well as the behavioral sciences and anthropology. Many teachers choose to ground their social studies lessons and units in one discipline, often history. Finally, the third component of social studies is its purpose—the education of citizens. In short, we learn for a higher purpose and that purpose is to fulfill our responsibilities as citizens. This can be challenging for elementary students who often believe that the purpose of their learning is to perform on a test. While we operate from this understanding of social studies, we should also note that this definition is not accepted by everyone in social studies. The rejection comes in part from those who believe that the components of integration and civic competence in the definition detract from the purity of the social science disciplines of history, political science, geography, and economics, among others, and dilutes the purpose of learning, as well as the actual learning of any of the fields (Ravitch, 2000). Although we appreciate this concern, we believe that the integrity of the disciplines can be preserved, and even seen as more relevant, when integrated effectively and for the purpose of civic life.

Education for the purpose of citizenship includes an examination of the rights and responsibilities of citizenship, the understanding of citizenship in terms of both status (legal and procedural) and practice (way of life), its historical and philosophical foundations, as well as knowledge of current laws and public policy (Niemi, Sanders, & Whittington, 2005; Weiss, Lutkus, Grigg, & Niemi, 2001). Within social studies, civic education also addresses the importance of competencies or skills. According to Torney-Purta (2002), "Schools achieve the best results in fostering civic engagement when they rigorously teach civic content and skills . . ." (p. 203). These skills include intellectual or cognitive skills, commonly referred to as critical thinking and higher order thinking skills (Patrick, 1999). This includes the ability to describe, analyze, and interpret information from a wide variety of sources. In addition to intellectual skills, Patrick (1999) and Hess (2008), note the importance of participatory skills that help students effectively engage and communicate in civic life. Finally, an educated citizenry possesses certain democratic dispositions and displays a democratic character, and represents the beliefs and attitudes that contribute to a democratic tradition, including valuing justice, the equality and dignity of each individual, diversity, respecting and protecting individual rights for all, and the protection and promotion of the public good (Patrick, 1999). A person who holds the basic components of an educated democratic citizen possesses knowledge about his or her rights and responsibilities in society. In addition, he or she is disposed to preserve those rights and responsibilities for self and others, and has the requisite competencies necessary to work toward the preservation of a democratic society. However, it is important to note that these components may or may not take on a critical perspective personally or when enacted in the classroom (Tyson, 2003). That is, the particular content, skills, and dispositions we choose to teach our students and how we teach them may or may not take on a critical perspective.

Westheimer and Kahne (2004) developed a framework that described three types of citizens—personally responsible, participatory, and justice-oriented.

Only the justice-oriented citizen takes on a critical perspective because civic engagement occurs within the context of promoting social change by working with others in examining and working to change systems and institutions that oppress the natural and political rights of others. For example, elementary students may learn that good citizens follow the rules; following the rules makes them personally responsible. But, what if the rules are bad? What if they take away the rights of others? In those situations, being personally responsible is not enough. Participatory citizens in a sixth-grade class may volunteer once a semester to serve lunch at a homeless shelter. That is a good thing to do; it helps the community. But, according to Westheimer and Kahne, it does not go far enough because the cause of homelessness in the community is not examined. It does not ask what we can do to end homelessness. Another way to promote a more critical perspective in civic education is to incorporate multicultural democratic citizenship education. Parker (1996, 2001) and Marri (2003) note that multicultural democratic citizenship education provides specific attention to the necessity of diversity, membership in small and large publics, and the treatment of democracy as a path, not as a completed journey. Note that in this description, diversity is addressed as something more than an existing condition in society. Diversity is an asset and is necessary for healthy democracies. Further, to preserve and promote this asset, individuals are members of many communities or publics. The largest public is their membership as residents and citizens of the United States. This large public is also the only legalistic membership. Our citizenship or residency is linked to the nation, not to our state or city of residence. The state and city are two types of small publics that also have civic goals. We also belong to other types of small publics like ethnic communities, and even issues-based communities. Finally, this description also helps us remember that democracy is not achieved. As such, we are not done with our work. Democracy is a path that we continue to walk, finding new opportunities and realities that will help us redefine democratic societies and the necessary citizenship education.

Literacy

Historically, literacy has been closely related to democracy, as Graff (1987) states, "the Western tradition of an educated electorate, schooling in literacy as preparation for citizenship, and the equation of literacy and democracy were born [in Athens, Greece]" (p. 23). Centuries later, early literacy goals in the United States were aligned with definitions of literacy congruent with learning to read and write in order to become good citizens (Smith, 1896), as a means of assimilation (Graff, 1987), and as a mechanism for establishing an educated workforce (Guerra, 1998). In many ways, these definitions of literacy can be seen as functional. Functional literacy is bound by the needs and expectations for competency in particular settings (Scribner, 1984). Often it is relegated to a skills and task type of view of literacy, decontextualized and focused on testing in a scientific or objective manner, or involving basic literacy tasks such as completing forms, which depict only a rudimentary level of literacy (Lytle, 1991). Narrowing literacy down to skills such as reading and retelling texts verbatim can prevent in-depth understanding and application of the content read. Reading simply to perform simplistic tasks is important, but in order to be a part of society individuals must be able to read for their own purposes and evaluate information in order to make decisions. Functional literacy instruction can create semiliterate and functionally literate individuals. Macedo (1993) describes the semiliterate individual as someone who may be well read in one area but unable to "read the world" or apply their knowledge outside of one area, while a functional literate is one "groomed primarily to meet the requirements of our contemporary society" (p. 189). The historian Graff states, "The schools have never attempted to provide more than 'basic,' 'functional' literacy abilities. Literacy has never, in Western history, been concerned with providing a grounding in skills that were expected to be developed into higher, self-advancing critical tools." (1987, p. 397). Education can be described as maintaining the status quo, ensuring that students are educated in order to serve the society's needs as determined by the institutions of schooling. At the other end of the spectrum lies critical literacy. Critical literacy can be viewed as a "political commitment to democratic and emancipatory forms of education" (McLaren & Lankshear, 1993, p. 380). Critical literacy strives to educate students beyond functional basic skills so they can participate, evaluate, and shape their worlds. Today, the conceptual understandings of literacy, (e.g., critical literacy, multiliteracies) continue to evolve (Janks, 2000) and press past the boundaries of reading and writing. Within these expanding areas lay the intricate distinctions of literacy in relation to culture (Clark & Flores, 2007; Freire & Macedo, 1987; Heath, 1983; McMillon & McMillon, 2004), to personal fulfillment (Guerra, 1998), to power and social justice (Morrell, 2007; Scribner, 1984), and to personal achievement and national issues (Arnove & Graff, 2001; Collins & Blot, 2003; Luke, 2000). While these conceptions of civic education and literacy thrive in some educational contexts and in theory, they have been constrained by policy movements during the past decade. Whereas literacy began as a functional tool for citizens to participate in democratic societies, today the retreat back to functional literacy connotes a reduction back to fundamentals out of apprehension rather than necessity.

Barriers to Educating Our Developing Citizens

Our current work in schools is insufficient for the preservation and progress of a democratic United States. Our democracy will not survive, let alone thrive, simply because it is a political and social institution; it needs to advance and be supported by informed, resilient, and educated citizens. Unfortunately, we are teaching and our students are learning in elementary schools that are not teaching social studies because they are encased in a back-to-basics, one-size-fits-all, measurement-driven environment that places our students and our democracy at risk. There has been a crisis in the classroom founded on the current era bound by measurable skills pressed into discrete pieces of information to be tested (Association, 1999; Janesick, 2007). The accountability movement, and schools' subsequent implementation decisions, have led to time constraints (e.g., 90-minute literacy block) protecting some disciplines (e.g., literacy and math) at the expense of others, specifically social studies (Howard, 2003; VanFossen, 2005; Vogler, et al, 2007). High-stakes test-driven pedagogies do not measure conceptual or complex knowledge or critical thinking; they focus on recall and comprehension only in particular subjects, and are completely insufficient for the education of citizens. Amid calls for twenty-first century literacies (Kallus, 2011) enacted within a global society (Blackburn & Clark, 2007; Street, 2004), institutional, oversimplified education requires contraction and simplification of ideas and fails to attend to the sociocultural, political, and historical context of the twenty-first century.

The Accountability Era: Civic Education and Literacy in Elementary Schools

No Child Left Behind (NCLB) brought high-stakes testing to elementary schools (Kornhaber, 2004). Both civic education and literacy education in the United States have been subject to the existing policy-based test-driven environment and thus woefully inadequate in preparing the kind of citizens required by our democracy. While literacy has been relegated to a simplistic functional view that seeks to measure low-level skills rather than critical thinking and multiple literacies (Behrman, 2006; Tierney, 2008), civic education (as a component of the social studies curriculum) is either completely missing from numerous schools in favor of more time for a test-driven math and literacy curriculum (Fitchett & Heafner, 2010; VanFossen, 2005; Wills, 2007) or relegated to the recall of basic information (Vogler & Virtue, 2007). Literacy instruction was guided by policies that served as backseat drivers for instructional practices and assessments. As Calfee states,

> . . . in 2002 as NCLB, the federal government instituted programs of standardized testing and school-level accountability that now significantly influence "what counts"—what is taught, how it is taught, and how it is assessed. The greatest impact of NCLB has been on reading instruction in the elementary grades (2014, p. 1).

The focus on high-stakes testing pressured teachers to teach to the test and focus on ensuring that students were competent in multiple choice test formats, thus removing aspects of critical thinking and moving to lower level skills. The use of programmatic instruction became the norm for most teachers as they were required to adhere to teacher proof scripts and constant assessments.

As the literacy curriculum narrowed, schools had little to no time available for social studies, including civic education. There are numerous reasons for this, most notably accountability pressures. States, school districts, and administrators are requiring and monitoring extended blocks of time devoted to math and literacy. Further, as many schools adopt packaged math and literacy curricula, some of it heavily scripted, teachers find that deviating from a script is an additional barrier to the possibility of integrating social studies into mandated literacy and math blocks of time. While some teachers bemoan the loss of social studies, others are less troubled because of their own discomfort teaching social studies. For many, social studies is seen as a boring and irrelevant subject (Goodlad, 1984); and, given how it is often taught, as a distant and disconnected set of facts with no relevance to the current world of the student or society, Goodlad's findings are not surprising. Further, eliminating social studies or reconceptualizing it as an all-encompassing academic subject has made what limited space there was for social studies now the place for many supplemental programs and curricula such as drug awareness and school assemblies. Categorizing these experiences as social studies makes it easier to preserve dedicated time for more easily defined and/or tested subjects. The accountability era, accompanied by these additional issues, may have a negative impact on citizenship education.

As levels of education, which include civic-related content knowledge, have increased over time, the youth vote remains low (Burden, 2009; CIRCLE, 2006), as do many other forms of civic engagement (CIRCLE, 2006). This lack of engagement is related to a number of factors, including youth definitions of civic and political engagement (e.g., social networking, volunteerism) differing from traditional models (e.g., voting), as well as more troubling factors such as a disjuncture between what youth were taught about civic and political life and what they experienced in their daily lives (Rubin, 2007). For example, to learn that being a good citizen includes following the law, and then to see elected officials at the local and national levels violate the law is a disappointment. To learn that the 14th Amendment promises equal protection under the law, while witnessing almost daily occurrences of family and community members not offered equal protection—because of age, race, ethnicity, sexual orientation, or socioeconomic status—is more than a disappointment. While our elementary students are not yet voters, civic education cannot wait until their last years of high school. The requisite knowledge, skills, and dispositions must be addressed from kindergarten on. Teaching the complex and abstract ideas found in the social studies disciplines, as well as critical literacy, has the potential to empower our students in numerous ways, including in their civic lives.

The Current Standards Movements

The current standards movement led by the Common Core State Standards (CCSS) continues to concentrate on just language arts and math, disregarding the content of both social studies and science. The CCSS for English/Language Arts (CCSS ELA) emphasize the reading of informational text in the content areas such as Literacy in History/Social Studies, Science, and Technical Subjects (http://www.corestandards.org/assets/CCSSI_ELAStandards.pdf) yet the CCSS ELA positions those subjects in service to literacy. While informational text can be about a social studies topic, the CCSS ELA are still centered on listening, speaking, reading, and writing skills in relation to social studies. The CCSS ELA state, "Beginning in grade 6, the literacy standards allow teachers of ELA, history/social studies ... to use their content area expertise to help students meet the particular challenges of reading, writing, speaking, listening, and language in their respective fields." Therefore, the standards remain dedicated to literacy skills not on content areas themselves, and call for teachers to rely on their knowledge of content.

In response to the exclusion of social studies from the CCSS, professional organizations representing social studies education and science education have recently created new standards prioritizing their content areas that are compatible with the CCSS ELA. The National Council for the Social Studies (NCSS), the national professional organization representing social studies educators, recently created *Social Studies for the Next Generation: Purposes, Practices, and Implications of the College, Career, and **Civic Life*** [emphasis added] *(C3) Framework for Social Studies State Standards* (NCSS, 2013) that provide explicit attention to four key disciplinary areas within social studies (i.e., civics, economics, geography, history), situated within the purpose of citizenship education, and complementary to both the CCSS ELA standards and the NCSS Curriculum Standards (2010). Note that the title of these new standards brings civics into a place of prominence, along with the CCSS focus on career and college. It should also be noted that the C3 Framework is not a content standards document. Rather, the C3 Framework focuses on the process of inquiry and the development of disciplinary inquiry skills across the social studies. More specific social studies curriculum and content standards are available in the 2010 NCSS Curriculum Standards that focus on social studies concepts, the voluntary national standards created by separate social science disciplines (e.g., the National Standards for Civics and Government, National Standards in Economics, National History Standards, National Geography Standards & Skills), as well as the local content standards developed in most states. For our purposes and in this book, we rely on the CCSS ELA and the C3 Framework for Social Studies. As you spend time with the detailed lessons in Chapters 3–6, you will note that they are aligned with these two standards documents. We know that not all states have adopted the CCSS and the C3 Framework standards so we encourage you to use the standards that are required in your school setting. Two additional sources for standards are the NCSS Curriculum Standards and the International Reading Association, and we provide an overview of those standards in Chapter 7. We believe that the current standards movements open up the possibility of a return to the integration of social studies and literacy. While not all states adopted the CCSS, and some early adopters have since dropped the CCSS, the structure and content of the standards is influencing many standards in place and in development. Some of those states that have dropped the CCSS have created new standards that are very similar to the CCSS (see for example http://blogs.edweek.org/edweek/state_edwatch/2014/04/indiana_finally_adopts_standards_to_replace_common-core_adoption.html). We view integration as a way to bring social studies back into the elementary classroom in the current standards and accountability movements.

Integrating Social Studies and Literacy in the Elementary Classroom

Despite the various policy omissions and separations of social studies and literacy instruction, there has been a long tradition of integrating school subjects in American classrooms (Cremin, 1964; Langer & Allington, 1992). In the classroom, a teacher "... highlights the integration of content by blending disciplines through 'overlapping skills, concepts and attitudes'" (Fogarty, 1991b, p. 64, as cited in Gavelek, Raphael, Biondo, & Wang, 2000, p. 591). Curriculum integration was heavily advocated through the mid-1990s, but the test-driven programs of the NCLB era narrowed the curriculum in scope and content in the early years of the twenty-first century as teachers and schools were under extreme pressure to provide high test scores (Darling-Hammond, 2004). The more recent standards (i.e., CCSS), while still focused only on English/language arts and math include a specific section of standards titled *Literacy in History/Social Studies, Science, and Technical Subjects* (http://www.corestandards.org/assets/CCSSI_ELA%20Standards.pdf). These standards, while not including these content areas, acknowledge that learning these content areas requires literacy, and becoming literate requires knowledge of these content areas. This supports not just the idea of integration, but the necessity of integration based on expertise in all of the areas being integrated. While some (e.g., Hinde, 2005) see curriculum integration as a way to return social studies back to the elementary classroom, others (e.g., Brophy & Alleman, 2008) express concern that unless integration is implemented beyond a superficial understanding, science and social studies will still not be addressed in a way that attends to essential content, concepts, and skills in science and social studies. For example, many teachers use social studies content, such as Rosa Parks's actions, to supplement the literacy lesson when social studies content appears in informational text materials (e.g., textbooks) or in narrative texts (e.g., picture books) used for reading instruction. This orientation, while helpful for reading lesson instruction, is not social studies instruction. However, if teachers shift their focus from literacy and highlight social studies lessons they may struggle with trying to teach both facts and concepts. Often in social studies instruction, discussing and comprehending abstract concepts such as civil disobedience are sacrificed for the teaching of facts, such as memorizing that Rosa Parks was arrested in 1955 for not moving from her seat. When the facts are taught in isolation and disconnected from concepts that apply to students' lives, opportunities for meaningful learning and transfer are missed. In this typical model, teachers can find themselves having to choose to focus on literacy or social studies and may find they are not doing either one in-depth. In short, having students read a biography of Rosa Parks and asking only literacy comprehension questions does not address the goals and objectives of social studies. However, if students are asked questions that are grounded in civic concepts like civil disobedience and civic virtue, or historical thinking concepts (http://www.historicalthinking.ca/historical-thinking-concepts) such as taking historical perspectives and analyzing cause and consequence, we are moving toward more meaningful integration and better learning in both literacy and social studies. Therefore, throughout this book, there are units and lessons that model the integration of historical and civic knowledge from a critical perspective through critical literacy. As Levstik (2008) notes, "In order for literary texts to meet social studies' aims and purposes, the existing research suggests that teacher mediation is essential. Without purposeful attention to how texts are constructed, to alternative perspectives, and analysis of the social studies content as well as the literary merit of particular texts, students are likely to misconstrue social studies content" (p. 57). That is, without explicitly addressing the content and purposes of each of the disciplines being integrated, misconceptions occur. Our book is part of that "purposeful attention," providing explicit attention to both the content and pedagogy of both disciplines.

From a literacy perspective, the relationship between literacy instruction and content area instruction is currently under debate with content area reading (CAR) and disciplinary literacy being examined as both similar and separate ideas (Brozo, Moorman, Meyer, & Stewart, 2013; Hynd-Shanahan, 2013). CAR, in existence for decades but prevalent since the 1980s, focused on the ways in which content area teachers could assist students as they read informational texts and subject area textbooks (Stewart-Dore, 2013). CAR is dependent on specific teaching strategies to access texts across any content area. On the other hand, disciplinary literacy privileges the discipline first and then applies the strategies of the discipline (Hynd-Shanahan, 2013). In order to implement a disciplinary literacy approach, collaboration with disciplinary experts is essential. While there is debate and discussion, mostly concentrated on the secondary classroom, regarding what the relationship between a content area, such as social studies, and literacy instruction entails, our work focuses on integrated instruction at the elementary level.

Recognizing the challenge of moving social studies back into the elementary classroom in the accountability climate, the goal of this book is to bridge content area integration and literacy instruction with a critical reflective eye on conceptual mastery of social studies and critical literacy while recognizing that, "Integrated instruction is hard work that involves crossing boundaries of the curriculum and the classroom/school, involves intensive planning, and involves well-developed knowledge" (Gavelek, Raphael, Biondo, & Wang, 2000, p.600). Therefore, throughout the book we emphasize how elementary teachers can build up their content knowledge, pedagogical, curricular, and strategic knowledge (Shulman, 1986) in order to integrate social studies and literacy for elementary students beginning in kindergarten. We rest our work on the following three premises:

- It is not enough for teachers and their students to understand the components of democracy.
  - Many teachers and students may recall and know the political, social, and institutional dimensions of democracy, such as the three branches of government, but their understanding is superficial and/or their connection to the ideals of a democratic state are tenuous, leading to low, individualistic, and superficial levels of civic participation.
- It is not enough for teachers and their students to be literate.
  - Many teachers and students are functionally literate and are able to read and write, but this does not equate to highly or critically literate engaged individuals.
- It is not enough for teachers and their students to be critical.
  - Many teachers and students are critical, but their criticism and critiques are grounded in personal experiences or anecdotal accounts without consideration of multiple perspectives, and they are left mired in the continual reification of preexisting ideas.

Teachers and their students, as part of the "governed," should be informed and resilient enough to access and evaluate the overwhelming amount of constantly evolving and frequently conflicting information available today in order to provide informed consent for their own governance. Therefore, if all students are to become informed, resilient participants in our multifaceted democratic society, they must be taught by teachers who possess CDL.

References

Alexander, J., Walsh, P., Jarman, R., & McClune, B. (2008). From rhetoric to reality: advancing literacy by cross-curricular means. *The Curriculum Journal*, 19(1), 23–35.

Brophy, J. & Alleman, J. (2008). Early elementary social studies. In L. S. Levstik & C. A. Tyson (Eds.), *Handbook of research in social studies education* (pp. 33–49). New York, NY: Routledge.

Brozo, W. G., Moorman, G., Meyer, C., & Stewart, T. (2013). Content area reading and disciplinary literacy: A case for the radical center. *Journal of Adolescent & Adult Literacy*, 56(5) 353–357.

Calfee, R. C. (2014). Introduction—Knowledge, evidence, and faith: How the federal government used science to take over public schools. In K. S. Goodman, R. C. Calfee, & Y. M. Goodman (Eds.), *Whose knowledge counts in government literacy polices? Why expertise matters* (pp. 1–17). New York, NY: Routledge.

CIRCLE. (2006). *The 2006 civic and political health of the nation. A detailed look at how youth participate in politics and communities.* College Park, MD: CIRCLE.

Darling-Hammond, L. (2004). Standards, accountability, and school reform. *Teachers College Record*, 42, 75–83.

Dewey, J. (1944). *Democracy and education.* New York, NY: The Free Press.

Engle, S. H. & Ochoa, A. (1988). *Education for democratic citizenship: Decision-making in the social studies.* New York, NY: Teachers College Press.

Fendler, L. (1998). What is it impossible to think? A genealogy of the educated subject. In T. S. Popkewitz & M. Brennan (Eds.), *Foucault's challenge: Discourse, knowledge, and power in education* (pp. 39–63). New York, NY: Teachers College Press.

Gavelek, J. R., Raphael, T. E., Biondo, S. M., & Wang, D. (2000). Integrated literacy instruction. In M. Kamil, P. Mosenthal, P. D. Pearson, & R. Barr (Eds.), *Handbook of reading research: Vol. III.* Mahwah, NJ. Lawrence Erlbaum Associates.

Goodlad, J. I. (1984). *A place called school: Prospects for the future.* New York, NY: McGraw-Hill Book Co.

Hess, D. (2008). Democratic education to reduce the divide. *Social Education*, 72(7), 373–376.

Hinde, E. T. (2005). Revisiting curriculum integration: A fresh look at an old idea. *The Social Studies*, 96(3), 105–111.

Howard, R. (2003). The shrinking of social studies. *Social Education*, 67, 285–288.

Hynd-Shanahan, C. (2013). What does it take? The challenge of disciplinary literacy. *Journal of Adolescent & Adult Literacy*, 57(2), 93–98.

Ichilov, O. (2011). Privatization and commercialization of public education: Consequences for citizenship and citizenship education. *Urban Review*, 44, 281–301.

International Reading Association. (1999). High-stakes assessments in reading: A position statement of the International Reading Association. *Journal of Adolescent & Adult Literacy*, 43(3), 305–312.

Kornhaber, M. K. (2004). Appropriate and inappropriate forms of testing, assessment, and accountability. *Educational Policy*, 18(1) 45–70.

Levstik, L. S. (2008). What happens in social studies classrooms? In L. S. Levstik & C. A. Tyson (Eds.), *Handbook of research in social studies education* (pp. 50–62). New York, NY: Routledge.

Macedo, D. P. (1993). Literacy for stupidification: The pedagogy of big lies. *Harvard Educational Review*, 63(2) 183–206.

McLaren, P. L. & Lankshear, C. (1993). Critical literacy and the postmodern turn. In P. L. McLaren & C. Lankshear (Eds.), *Critical literacy: Politics, praxis, and the postmodern* (pp. 379–419). Albany, NY: SUNY Press.

National Council for the Social Studies. (2010). *National curriculum standards for social studies: A framework for teaching, learning, and assessment.* Silver Spring, MD: Author.

National Council for the Social Studies. (2013). *Social studies for the next generation: Purposes, practices, and implications of the college, career, and civic life (C3) framework for social studies state standards.* Silver Spring, MD: Author.

National Governors Association Center for Best Practices & Council of Chief State School Officers (NGA & CSSO). (2010). *Common Core State Standards for English language arts and literacy in history/social studies, science, and technical subjects.* Washington, DC: Authors.

Niemi, R. G., Sanders, M. S., & Whittington, D. (2005). Civic knowledge of elementary and secondary school students, 1933–1998. *Theory and Research in Social Education,* 33(2), 172–199.

Parker, W. C. (1996). "Advanced" ideas about democracy: Toward a pluralistic conception of citizen education. *Teachers College Record,* 98(1), 105–125.

Parker, W. C. (2001). Toward enlightened political engagement. In W. B. Stanley (Ed.), *Critical issues in social studies research for the 21st century* (pp. 97–118). Greenwich, CT: Information Age Publishing.

Patrick, J. J. (1999). Concepts at the core of education for democratic citizenship. In C. F. Bahmueller & J. J. Patrick (Eds.), *Principles and practices of education for democratic citizenship: International perspectives and projects* (pp. 1–40). Bloomington, IN: ERIC Clearinghouse for Social Studies/Social Science Education.

Pingree, S., Hawkins, R., & Renee, A. (2000). The effect of family communication patterns on young people's science literacy. *Science Communication,* 22(2) 115–132.

Ravitch, D. (2000). The educational backgrounds of history teachers. In P. N. Stearns, P. Seixas, & S. Wineburg (Eds.), *Knowing teaching & learning history: National and international perspectives* (pp. 143–155). New York, NY: New York University Press.

Scribner, S. (1984). Literacy in three metaphors, *American Journal of Education,* 93 (1) 6–21.

Shulman, L. S. (1986). Those who understand: Knowledge growth in teaching. *Educational Researcher,* 15(2), 4–14.

Torney-Purta, J. (2002). The school's role in developing civic engagement: A study of adolescents in twenty-eight countries. *Applied Developmental Science,* 6(4), 203–212.

Tyson, C. & Park, S. C. (2008). Civic education, social justice, and critical race theory. In J. Arthur, I. Davies, & C. Hahn (Eds.), *The SAGE handbook of education for citizenship and democracy* (pp. 29–39). Thousand Oaks, CA: SAGE Publications.

VanFossen, P. J. (2005). "Reading and math take so much of the time . . .": An overview of social studies instruction in elementary classrooms in Indiana. *Theory and Research in Social Education,* 33(3), 376–403.

Vogler, K. E. & Virtue, D. (2007). "Just the facts, Ma'am": Teaching social studies in the era of standards and high-stakes testing. *Social Studies,* 98(2), 54–58.

Vogler, K. E., Lintner, T., Lipscomb, G. B., Knopf, H., Heafner, T. L., & Rock, T. C. (2007). Getting off the back burner: Impact of testing elementary social studies as part of a state-mandated accountability program. *Journal of Social Studies Research,* 31(2), 20–34.

Westheimer, J. & Kahne, J. (2004). What kind of citizen? The politics of educating for democracy. *American Educational Research Journal,* 41(2), 237–269.

2
CRITICAL DEMOCRATIC LITERACY

Fostering Informed Resilient Engagement in a Democratic Society

In the preface, we provided an overview of the purpose and organization of the book, while Chapter 1 provided the rationale for our writing of it. Part of that rationale is our commitment to the development of citizens who possess, what we term, *Critical Democratic Literacy* (CDL). The development of CDL requires a refocus in K–6 education to prepare students for resilient democratic engagement in an ever-evolving and complex democratic society. We advocate preparing students, beginning in kindergarten, to engage in our increasingly complex and advanced version of democracy with a type of literacy necessary for comprehending and thinking critically about their civic lives from an informed stance; with resiliency and a disposition toward understanding and evaluating not only others' thoughts, but also evaluating their own; and where students move from a stance of certainty based on personal opinion and belief to a stance of reasoned, rational, and informed thought. This chapter introduces you to CDL by defining it, explaining the philosophical and disciplinary roots of CDL, and providing a rationale for CDL's necessity as part of the elementary literacy and social studies curricula. We also share examples of how citizens who possess CDL participate in society. The three distinct and interrelated components of CDL—critical, democracy, and literacy—are important to understand independently as well as how they work together. We begin with the concept of critical. This is followed by a discussion of democracy, including critical approaches to democracy. Finally, we define critical literacy and its relationship to democratic engagement.

What Does It Mean to Be *Critical* in Critical Democratic Literacy?

The *critical* in CDL is a distinct concept and it also represents a specific perspective for how we define both democracy and literacy. Our critical stance is based on Critical Theory, a philosophy and theoretical perspective that was developed about a century ago in Europe. A complex array of scholars and perspectives exist within Critical Theory but basically Critical Theory is a perspective focused on examining power relationships (Giroux, 1980; Kincheloe, 2004). Critical Theory seeks to understand and, if necessary, disrupt the status quo by searching for information from multiple viewpoints with an eye toward power relationships between and within individuals, institutions, and societies. There is a separate role for Critical Theory in education and this frames the critical in CDL. Educational experiences should make students aware of injustice, particularly at systemic and institutional levels, past and present. This could include how local and federal laws kept African American citizens from voting and female citizens from owning property as past examples, as well as more current concerns that new voter ID laws place an unfair or unjust burden on our poor and elderly citizens who have the right to vote. Note that these discussions of injustice go well beyond individual actions and instead focus on the unjust policies, laws, and actions of powerful institutions like governments, educational and medical institutions, and even informal institutions that we may think of as "traditions" or "that is just the way we have always done it." Whether formal or informal, these policies, practices, and traditions may lead to, and perpetuate, unjust policies, practices, and traditions. In addition to an awareness of injustice, education should help students develop an awareness of and understanding of power, and learn to recognize abuses of power, whether that be abuses by the formerly pro-Apartheid government of South Africa, the Taliban's restriction of girls' education in Pakistan, or US business's child labor practices in the early twentieth century. An important goal for our students in recognizing injustice and the use of power to perpetuate injustice is for them to see patterns to the injustice and abuse of power across institutions, across time (i.e., through history), and across space (i.e., local, national, and global.) In a critical perspective, once our students develop this awareness, we should help them to recognize their individual and collective power to work against injustice and to make their communities better for all residents. The desire to work against injustice is closely tied to the ideals of democracy and a civic education that supports democratic institutions.

What Does *Democratic* Mean in Critical Democratic Literacy?

Democratic in CDL is an acknowledgement that the primary purpose of public schooling in the United States is citizenship education (Dewey, 1944; Gutmann, 1987; Parker, 2001). Given that the United States is a democracy (i.e., democratic republic, representative democracy), school curricula and accompanying instructional practices should include certain knowledge, skills and/or competencies, and dispositions and/or character consistent with certain characteristics and ideals of democracy. It is reasonable to expect that the United States, which promotes itself at home and abroad as a beacon of democracy, would have a particular kind of education for democracy, whether that be a democratic school structure, formal citizenship education courses, social studies courses, or more informally as part of a school's mission or climate. The education of the citizenry in a democracy is somewhat complicated by varying interpretations of democracy (e.g., Barber's 1984 discussion of strong democracy vs. thin democracy is one discussion of different interpretations) and of democratic ideals. Current understandings of American democracy typically include ideals and concepts such as justice, human rights, equality, liberty, and the consent and right of the governed to dissent (Dahl, 1998). That is not to say that everyone defines these ideals and concepts the same way and that can make teaching, learning, and living democratically challenging. Let us think about the concept of justice as an example. John Rawls (1971) wrote about the concept of justice, defining justice as fairness: everyone is equal before the law and everyone has the same opportunity to be successful, however they define success. He believed that our context (e.g., our history, economic status, race, sex) did not matter. However, Iris Marion Young (1990), another philosopher who approached democracy from a more critical perspective, wrote that as nice as it would be for context to not matter, it does. As a result, not everyone in society has an equal opportunity to succeed and there continues to be a lot of institutional injustice that needs to be fixed. And, because we live in a democracy, we, the people, are responsible for coming together and creating a more just United States for ourselves and for others. So, Rawls and Young and many others may be in agreement that justice is an important ideal and essential concept in understanding democracy. However, the concept of justice is not understood by everyone in the same way.

These varied understandings of the core ideals of democracy result in societies and schools translating and teaching democracy, including the ideal of justice, in different ways. Given this, there are multiple visions of what democratic education (Biesta, 2010; Gutmann, 1987), civic education (Ehrlich,1999; Hughes, Print, & Sears, 2010; Patrick, 1999), and democratic citizenship education (Engle & Ochoa, 1988; Knight Abowitz & Harnish, 2006; Marciano, 1997; Ruitenberg, 2009; Tyson & Park, 2008; Westheimer & Kahne, 2004) should include and how they should be taught. Consistent with our inclusion of a *critical* perspective as part of CDL, our vision of citizenship education requires an understanding of democracy that, for example, includes the belief that justice cannot be achieved without recognition of the need for collective action to mitigate unequal opportunities. Even with these varied and contested understandings of some of the ideals and concepts of democracy and an accompanying education, there is a shared belief that education for democracy is necessary in a society that purports to need informed and engaged participation (McDonnell, 2000; Parker, 2001). Part of the responsibility of being an informed and engaged citizen is the responsibility to be literate. Like democracy, literacy in CDL is framed through a critical perspective.

What Is Critical *Literacy* and How Does It Fit Into Critical Democratic Literacy?

Constructions and definitions of literacy in relation to education are varied and complex and range from viewing literacy as specific "skills and tasks" (Lytle, 1991, p. 110) to multiple literacies as a broad understanding of a particular field of knowledge and distributed via various modes and types of texts (Gee, 2009; Kress, 2005; Leu, Kinzer, Coiro, & Cammack, 2004; Mills, 2010; Siegel, 2006; The New London Group, 1996) to critical literacy (Endres, 2001; Freire, 2000; Luke, 2008; Morrell, 2007). The *literacy* of CDL relies on notions of critical literacy as described by Lytle:

> . . . literacy [is defined] as a process of critical reflection and action: a process of interpreting the world and developing a consciousness of values, behaviors, and beliefs as socially and culturally constructed. Frequently cited exemplars of literacy as critical reflection include Freire's (1983) notion of "reading the word" in order to "read the world," and Giroux's (1983) concept of literacy as a critical decoding of ones' own experiences in order to make problematic one's assumptions and perceptions of the world. For adult learners, then, literacy may involve posing as well as solving problems, so that an index of individual and group literacy development would be their more deliberate use of social, cultural, economic, and political lenses to decode the world (1991, p. 116).

We adapt Lytle's ideas about critical literacy within the knowledge of democratic/citizenship education. This is in contrast to literacy viewed as a means of democratic participation as measured by a functional literacy that serves only superficial participatory activities such as filling out voting forms or as situated in an integrated system (McGuire, 2007; Paquette & Kaufman, 2008). In other words, we advocate preparing students to engage in the twenty-first century's increasingly complex democracy with a type of literacy necessary for comprehending and thinking critically about their civic engagement from an informed stance, with resiliency and the ability to evaluate others' thoughts and views, as well as their own. Highly literate students should be able to move from a stance of certainty based on personal opinion and belief to a stance of reasoned, rational, and informed thought. We conceptualize CDL as a particular type of literacy similar to conceptions of mathematical literacy, financial literacy, or scientific literacy as described by Alexander, Walsh, Jarman, and McClune (2008):

> Science-literate people are those who do some basic evaluation of sources of information, understand enough about the processes of science to believe that it is useful, apply that understanding to the news stories they read and hear, and can interpret and place the information they receive into a context that is meaningful and useful to their own lives (Pingree, Hawkins, & Renee, 2000) ... scientific literacy is important because of the nature of today's society (p. 25).

As a type of literacy, CDL relies on the disciplinary foundational knowledge that democratic/citizenship education provides. This disciplinary knowledge is typically found in the social studies (i.e., political science/civics, history, geography, economics) and this disciplinary focus moves literacy beyond a simple reliance just on reading and writing. In sum, each of the three key ideas of CDL—*critical, democracy,* and *literacy*—are defined in ways that challenge superficial, functional, and simplistic understandings. Similarly, citizens who are critically democratically literate think and act in ways that challenge these simplistic understandings. But what might that look like? For that, we turn to an explanation and example of CDL in practice.

What Does a Citizen Who Is Critically Democratically Literate Look Like?

Individuals who possess CDL are those who are knowledgeable about democracy as a concept, and who demonstrate their civic virtue by committing to engage in civic and political life in ways that support democratic ideals for all residents of the nation. Sometimes this means challenging powerful institutions, long-standing traditions, and even unjust laws as citizens work to achieve those ideals. This may include engaging in civil disobedience because powerful institutions and traditions usually resist changing, especially if these institutions would lose power and privileges as a result of those changes. These citizens are able to critically comprehend, evaluate, and navigate innumerable types of information related to democratic ideals from social, cultural, economic, and political perspectives. Further, they understand and appreciate the process of civic engagement and apply that understanding as they contribute to civil discourse for the purpose of bettering society for self and others. CDL is important in the sense that citizens/students should be resilient enough to consistently engage in democratic life as they listen to and read news stories, interact with those in their community, and make decisions related to their democratic participation. Education for CDL builds a needed resiliency to navigate, understand, and evaluate political and civic information via new literacies in order to remain an engaged and informed participant in society. The development of such a citizen cannot wait until adulthood. The knowledge, skills, habits, and dispositions included require meaningful and frequent opportunities and experiences throughout students' educational lives.

What Does CDL Look Like in an Elementary Classroom?

In order to move beyond basic ideas of social studies and literacy education, we rely on work from the fields of social studies, democratic theories, and critical literacy to formulate a template for application in K–6 education, as well as for inclusion in teacher education. Teaching for CDL in the elementary classroom is feasible. It takes an informed, educated, and committed teacher, someone like first-grade teacher Michelle Findley who shared her reflection on a particular CDL lesson she taught to her students. Findley's work reflects the notion of teachers as "educated subject[s]" (Fendler, 1998, p. 55) who are able to create their own lessons and engage their students in rigorous conceptual discussions and activities.

> *Click, Clack, Moo: Cows That Type,* is a story that I have been using for the last 2 years as a means to teach letter writing. However, I used the Parker readings as inspiration this time to go deeper into content to teach what it means to be an enlightened and engaged citizen. I wanted the children in first grade to understand what it means to participate as a citizen in order to make society better for all. First, I used key vocabulary, "citizen, engaged, and strike." I gave them the developmentally appropriate definitions of "doing something" for engagement and "a person who lives in a town or a city," for citizen. At this level I needed to keep the definitions very basic as I will use the book as a bridge to scaffold to "engaged citizen." I used Parker's definition of "enlightened political engagement" as a model; "Wise participation or reflective involvement in civic affairs." In order to give this lesson, I needed to have the content knowledge necessary. I would not have been able to accomplish this without knowing the definitions of engagement, citizenship, and citizen. I have used this story before, but have only used it as a means to teach how to write a letter. In my past experiences with the restrictions of Reading First, I only taught vocabulary if it was directly used within the text. I had to stick to a specific script and was judged as to how closely I was able to follow it. Even though I was able to find time for bringing in another text, I did not understand how to bring thinking to a critical level, based on my training at the time. Through my many readings about engaged citizenship and citizenship education (particularly Parker), I was able to expand this reading to a more in depth study of what it means to be an engaged citizen.
>
> My group of first graders was engaged in a class discussion about what it means to be an engaged citizen as explained by Parker (2001), "A person who actively participates in society for the purpose of changing injustices and unfair practices." (p. 99). I read aloud the book, *Click, Clack, Moo: Cows That Type,* by Doreen Cronin [2000] ... I gave the goal for the story which was to think about citizens who are engaged. I started the read-aloud *Click,*

> *Clack, Moo: Cows That Type* . . . I asked, "What do you think the cows are doing?" and "Why?" as a means to have the students recognize that there was a problem that needed to be solved, and one way to do this was to write a letter. I therefore addressed civic education by having the students tell me that the cows were citizens and that the problem to be solved was that they were cold at night and the solution was to be given electric blankets. They were then able to see that the cows were "engaged citizens." This was also a good example of a "participatory citizen," as explained by Westheimer and Kahne (2004), "To solve social problems and improve society, citizens must actively participate and take leadership positions within established systems and community structures" (2004, p. 240). I was able to have the students think more critically than if they just memorized the vocabulary or answered comprehension questions. The students had to understand the cows' problem and recognize that the solution was to write a letter explaining the problem. After we shared and discussed, the students helped create a web that involved the things the animals did in the story to be engaged citizens. The children then moved to their desks and wrote letters as if they were other animals living on the farm that had a problem that needed to be solved. . . . I took the idea of engagement and related it to the playground and doing schoolwork so that they could then relate it to writing letters. I also asked them if they were citizens of the school to help them see the connection that the animals are citizens on the farm. In future lessons, I can use the book as an example and then use this as a bridge to citizens in a city or town.

Findley provides an example of how elementary teachers can begin to teach young students how to be informed and critically thinking citizens. Her lesson also offers insight into her powerful knowledge and control of her curriculum. Findley clearly discusses how her approach to using *Click, Clack, Moo: Cows That Type* (Cronin, 2000) dramatically changed as she learned about and committed to a meaningful integration of civic engagement with her literacy curriculum rather than a functional literacy approach focused on just the skill of letter writing. Findley also provides an example of the idea of *plus knowledge* in that she specifically notes that she needed to understand substantial additional content about civic education beyond what could be found in the text she was using. Highly educated teachers such as Findley alter the landscape of teaching as they use their knowledge to assist their students' development of CDL. Educated teachers can reconceptualize their teaching and become empowered as professionals. As Fendler (1998) states in her historical analysis of the educated subject ". . . power had been conceived as sovereign and outside of the self . . . The educated subject, then, became endowed with a new sort of power, namely, the power to govern itself" (p. 52). We borrow from Fendler's analysis of the educated subject to redefine educated teachers in relation to the policies and programs that seek to define their work. Educated teachers are not simply receivers of packaged programs; they are knowledgeable enough about CDL to both instruct and question the very disciplines they teach, empowering them to continue to move students into spaces for new imaginings of democracy beyond the bound prescribed conceptions. The accountability movements seek to contain and command an educational system that is perceived to be out of control, while restraining, admonishing, and deskilling (Apple & Teitelbaum, 1986) another generation of teachers. Teachers have been trained in systematic assembly line skills via programmatic instruction with professional development that reinforces the status quo with little means to become educated. In literacy, teachers and programs have been tightly focused on meeting high-stakes testing requirements that highlight easily measured aspects of reading and writing (Pennington, 2003). Social studies is not tested in the majority of states and rarely at the elementary level. When it is tested, social studies content is typically measured through basic recall of factual information (Au, 2009). Due to the climate of high-stakes testing, teacher and student knowledge is constructed as an overly simplistic set of skills and facts—facts that rely on a low-level fundamental view of what teachers and students can achieve. These notions are aligned with what Fendler (1998) describes as defining the "educated subject" (i.e., teachers) through objectifying their knowledge, "The 'nature' of the educated subject is stipulated in advance, based on objective criteria, usually statistical analysis . . . [where] the outcome drives the procedure" (p. 57). This reinforces the notion of training teachers rather than educating them. As schools continue to tighten, narrow, and segment the literacy and social studies curricula, moving further away from Dewey's (1944) ideal of school as an embryonic society, it is our responsibility to transform our practices. We posit that the only way to affect the sociopolitical context is to educate our teachers so their students will possess the resilient capacity to stay engaged in the political and civic process and provide their informed consent, which is necessary for a twenty-first century social contract.

We are not just integrating school subjects (i.e., literacy and social studies/civics); we are also integrating a critical perspective into each of these subjects in order to think about CDL as a complex whole. Unit plans that integrate civic education and literacy within a critical perspective can be designed to bring democracy to life for elementary students and assist them in understanding the concepts of participating (e.g., civic engagement), talking through problems and working together (e.g., civil discourse), being a good citizen (e.g., civic virtue), and standing up for your friends (e.g., civil disobedience). To aid in the development of CDL for young children, we propose utilizing four guiding civic concepts to frame an elementary CDL curriculum:

- Civic virtue
  - This requires that students recognize the relationship between individual rights and the necessity of working for the common good as they

participate in civic life experiences where not all individuals are afforded the same rights and privileges. K–6 educators understand the role of transformative praxis as a critical framework related to social justice for all.
- Civic engagement
  - This requires that students be connected to their world at the local, national, and international level in ways that necessitate the application of CDL knowledge, skills, and dispositions. K–6 educators embed opportunities for guided participation in civic life across disciplines in integrated ways that do not separate subject areas.
- Civil discourse
  - This requires that students participate regularly in civil discourse as they recognize how CDL knowledge, skills, and dispositions vary in application across differing sociocultural and historical contexts. K–6 educators acknowledge the complexity of today's world and provide students with the foundational knowledge and critical thinking and communication skills necessary for resilient engagement with others.
- Civil disobedience
  - This requires that students recognize unjust institutions, laws, and practices and how that injustice harms their individual lives and the broader society in which they live. K–6 educators create opportunities for students to explore ways they can participate, as citizens, in moving toward a more just world.

These four concepts provide a foundation for an elementary focus on civic education. A conceptual focus allows for building students' understandings beyond simple lessons; it promotes transfer of the conceptual beyond the classroom. While the following four chapters each address one of the four civic concepts, collectively these four civic concepts can frame each elementary grade's curriculum. CDL is not a skill set or a list of competencies; it is a deeply conceptual understanding of how to live within an ever-changing democratic society where information is consistently available and complex.

Why Should We Care About Critical Democratic Literacy?

Education for Critical Democratic Literacy builds a needed resiliency to navigate, understand, and evaluate political and civic information via new literacies in order to remain an engaged and informed participant in society. As schools continue to tighten, narrow, and segment the literacy and democratic/civic education curriculum, moving further away from Dewey's (1944) ideal of school as an embryonic society, it is our responsibility to transform our practices. We propose that teaching our students to see themselves as important members of their civic communities, dedicated to their communities' improvement, will result in a better and more just world for themselves and others.

In the next four chapters, we describe integrated social studies and literacy lessons in kindergarten, third, fourth, and fifth grades, all designed around CDL and the four civic concepts introduced in the preceding section. We also provide some insight into each teacher's decision-making, providing insight into their teacher content knowledge (Shulman, 1986). As you read the chapters, we ask you to reflect on:

- how the content and instruction of the lessons are focused on CDL;
- the ways in which social studies and literacy are integrated;
- how you might adapt CDL, social studies, literacy, and the specific content into your own context.

References

Addis, C. (2003). *Jefferson's vision for education, 1760–1845*. New York, NY: Peter: Lang Publishing, Inc.

Alexander, J., Walsh, P., Jarman, R., & McClune, B. (2008). From rhetoric to reality: Advancing literacy by cross-curricular means. *The Curriculum Journal*, 19(1), 23–35.

Apple, M. W. (2005). Patriotism, democracy, and the hidden effects of race. In C. McCarthy, W. Crichlow, G. Dimitriadis, & N. Dolby (Eds.), *Race, identity, and representation in education* (2nd ed.) (pp. 337–348). New York, NY: Routledge.

Arnove, R. F. & Graff, H. J. (2001). National literacy campaigns. In E. Cushman, E. R. Kingten, B. M. Kroll & M. Rose (Eds.), *Literacy: A critical sourcebook* (pp. 591–615). New York, NY: Bedford/St. Martin's.

Barber, B. (1984). *Strong democracy: Participatory politics for a new age*. Ewing, NJ: University of California Press.

Behrman, E. H. (2006). Teaching about language, power, and text: A review of classroom practices that support critical literacy. *Journal of Adolescent & Adult Literacy*, 49(6), 490–498.

Biesta, G. (2010). How to exist politically and learn from it: Hannah Arendt and the problem of democratic education. *Teachers College Record*, 112(2), 556–575.

Blackburn, M.V. & Clark, C.T. (2007). Bridging the local/global divide: Theorizing connections between global issues and local action. In M.V. Blackburn &C.T. Clark (Eds.), *Literacy research for political action and social change* (pp. 9–28). New York, NY: Peter Lang.

Burden, B. C. (2009). The dynamic effects of education on voter turnout. *Electoral Studies*, 28(4), 540–549.

CIRCLE. (2006). *The 2006 civic and political health of the nation: A detailed look at how youth participate in politics and communities*. College Park, MD: Author.

Clark, E. R. & Flores, B. B. (2007). Cultural literacy: Negotiating language, culture, and thought. *Voices from the Middle*, 15(2), 8–14.

Collins, J. & Blot, R. K. (2003). *Literacy and literacies: Texts, power, and identity*. New York, NY: Cambridge University Press.

Cronin, D. (2000). *Click, clack, moo: Cows that type*. New York, NY: Simon & Schuster.

Dahl, R. A. (1998). *On democracy*. New Haven, CT: Yale University Press.

Dewey, J. (1944). *Democracy and education*. New York, NY: The Free Press.

Ehrlich, T. (1999). Civic education: Lessons learned. *PS: Political Science and Politics*, 32(2), 245–250.

Endres, B. (2001). A critical read on critcal literacy: From critique to dialogue as an ideal for literacy education. *Educational Theory*, 51(4), 401–413.

Engle, S. & Ochoa, A. (1988). *Education for democratic citizenship: Decision-making in the social studies*. New York, NY: Teachers College Press.

Fendler, L. (1998). What is it impossible to think? A genealogy of the educated subject. In T. S. Popkewitz & M. Brennan, (Eds.), *Foucault's challenge: Discourse, knowledge, and power in education* (pp. 39–63). New York, NY: Teachers College Press.

Fitchett, P. G. & Heafner, T. L. (2010). A national perspective on the effects of high-stakes testing and standardization on elementary social studies marginalization. *Theory and Research in Social Education*, 38(1), 114–130.

Freire, P. (1983). The importance of the act of reading. *Journal of Education*, 165, 5–11.

Freire, P. (2000). *Pedagogy of the oppressed*. New York, NY: Continuum International Publishing Group.

Freire, P. & Macedo, D. (1987). *Literacy: Reading the word and the world*. South Hadley, MA: Bergin and Garvey.

Galston, W. (2001). Political knowledge, political engagement, and civic education. *Annual Review of Political Science*, 4, 217–234.

Gee, J. P. (2009). Reflections on reading Cope and Kalantzis' "'Multiliteracies': New Literacies, New Learning." *Pedagogies: An International Journal*, 4, 196–204.

Giroux, H. A. (1983). *Theory and resistance in education: A pedagogy for the opposition*. South Hadley, MA: Bergin & Garvey.

Giroux, H. A. (1980). Critical theory and rationality in citizenship education. *Curriculum Inquiry*, 10(4) 329–366.

Graff, H. J. (1987). *The legacies of literacy: Continuities and contradictions in western culture and society*. Indianapolis, IN: Indiana University Press.

Guerra, J. C. (1998). *Close to home: Oral and literate practices in a transnational Mexicano community*. New York, NY: Teachers College Press.

Gutmann, A. (1987). *Democratic education*. Princeton, NJ: Princeton University Press.

Heath, S. B. (1983). *Ways with words: Language, life, and work in communities and classrooms*. Cambridge, UK: Cambridge University Press.

Hess, D. (2008). Democratic education to reduce the divide. *Social Education*, 72(7), 373–376.

Hobbes, T. (1651/1968). *Leviathan*. London, UK: Penguin Classics.

hooks, b. (2010). *Teaching critical thinking: Practical wisdom*. New York, NY: Routledge.

Hughes, A. S., Print, M., & Sears, A. (2010). Curriculum capacity and citizenship education: A comparative analysis of four democracies. *Compare: A Journal of Comparative and International Education*, 40(3), 293–309.

International Reading Association (1999). High-stakes assessments in reading: A position statement of the International Reading Association. *Journal of Adolescent & Adult Literacy*, 43(3), 305–312.

Janesick, V. J. (2007). Reflections on the violence of high-stakes testing and the soothing nature of critical pedagogy. In P. McLaren & J. L. Kincheloe (Eds.), *Critical pedagogy: Where are we now?* (pp. 239–248). New York, NY: Peter Lang.

Janks, H. (2000). Domination, access, diversity and design: a synthesis for critical literacy education. *Educational Review*, 52(2), 175–186.

Kallus, M. K. (2011). What is text? A twenty-first century definition. In J. B. Cobb & M. K. Kallus (Eds.), *Historical, theoretical, and sociological foundations of reading in the United States* (pp. 71–78). New York, NY: Pearson.

Kennedy, J. J. (1997). Citizenship education in review: Past perspectives and future needs. In K. J. Kennedy (Ed.), *Citizenship education and the modern state* (pp.1–5). London, UK: Routledge Falmer.

Kincheloe, J. L. (2004). Critical pedagogy. New York, NY: Peter Lang.

Knight Abowitz, K. & Harnish, J. (2006). Contemporary discourses of citizenship. *Review of Educational Research*, 76(4), 653–690.

Kress, G. (2005). Gains and losses: New forms of texts, knowledge, and learning. *Computers and Composition*, 22(1), 5–22. doi: 10.1016/j.compcom.2004.12.004.

Leu, D. J., Jr., Kinzer, C. K., Coiro, J. L., & Cammack, D. W. (2004). Toward a theory of new literacies emerging from the Internet and other information and communication technologies. In R. B. Ruddell & N. J. Unrau (Eds.), *Theoretical models and processes of reading* (5th ed.). Newark, DE: International Reading Association.

Locke, J. (1960/1968). Two treatises of government. Cambridge, UK: Cambridge University Press.

Longo, N. V., Drury, C., & Battistoni, R. M. (2006). Catalyzing political engagement: Lessons for civic educators from the voices of students. *Annual Review of Political Science*, 2, 313–329.

Luke, A. (2000). Critical literacy in Australia: A matter of context and standpoint. *Journal of Adolescent & Adult Literacy*, 43(5), 448–461.

Luke, A. (2008). Using Bourdieu to make policy: Mobilizing community capital and literacy. In J. Albright & A. Luke (Eds.), *Pierre Bourdieu and literacy education* (pp. 347–362). New York, NY: Routledge.

Lytle, S. L. (1991). Living literacy: Rethinking development in adulthood. *Linguistics and Education*, 3, 109–138.

Marciano, J. (1997). *Civic illiteracy and education: The battle for the hearts and minds of American youth.* New York, NY: Peter Lang Publishing.

Marri, A. R. (2003). Multicultural democracy: Toward a better democracy. *Intercultural Education*, 14(3), 253–277.

McDonnell, L. M. (2000). Defining democratic purposes. In L. M. McDonnell, P. M. Timpane, & R. Benjamin (Eds.), *Rediscovering the democratic purposes of education* (pp. 1–18). Lawrence, KS: University Press of Kansas.

McGuire, M. (2007). What happened to social studies? The disappearing curriculum. *Phi Delta Kappan*, 620–624.

McMillon, G. T. & McMillon, V. D. (2004). The empowering literacy practices of an African American church. In F. B. Boyd, C. H. Brock, & M. S. Rozendal (Eds.), *Multicultural and multilingual literacy and language: Contexts and practices* (pp. 280–303). New York, NY: Guilford.

Mills, K. A. (2010). A review of the "digital turn" in the new literacy studies. *Review of Educational Research*, 80(2), 246–271. doi: 10.3102/0034654310364401.

Morrell, E. (2007). Critical literacy and popular culture in urban education: Toward a pedagogy of access and dissent. In M. V. Blackburn & C. T. Clark (Eds.), *Literacy research for political action and social change* (pp. 235–254). New York, NY: Peter Lang.

Niemi, R. G., Sanders, M. S., & Whittington, D. (2005). Civic knowledge of elementary and secondary school students, 1933–1998. *Theory and Research in Social Education*, 33(2), 172–199.

Paquette, K. R. & Kaufman, C. C. (2008). Merging civic literacy and literacy skills. *The Social Studies*, 187–190.

Parker, W. C. (1996). "Advanced" ideas about democracy: Toward a pluralistic conception of citizen education. *Teachers College Record*, 98(1), 105–125.

Parker, W. C. (2001). Toward enlightened political engagement. In W. B. Stanley (Ed.), *Critical issues in social studies research for the 21st century* (pp. 97–118). Greenwich, CT: Information Age Publishing.

Patrick, J. J. (1999). Concepts at the core of education for democratic citizenship. In C. F. Bahmueller & J. J. Patrick, (Eds.), *Principles and practices of education for democratic citizenship: International perspectives and projects* (pp. 1–40). Bloomington, IN: ERIC Clearinghouse for Social Studies/Social Science Education.

Pennington, J. L. (2003). Teaching interrupted: High-stakes testing in an inner city elementary school. In F. B. Boyd, C. H. Brock, & M. S. Rozendal (Eds.), *Multicultural and multilingual literacy and language practices: Constructing contexts for empowerment* (pp. 241–261). New York, NY: Guilford.

Pingree, S., Hawkins, R., & Renee, A. (2000). The effect of family communication patterns on young people's science literacy. *Science Communication*, 22(2), 115–132.

Rawls, J. (1971). *A theory of justice*. Cambridge, MA: President and Fellows of Harvard College.

Rousseau, J. (1968). *The social contract*. London, UK: Penguin Books.

Rubin, B. C. (2007). "There's still not justice": Youth civic identity development amid distinct school and community contexts. *Teachers College Record*, 109, 449–481.

Ruitenberg, C. W. (2009). Educating political adversaries: Chantal Mouffe and radical democratic citizenship education. *Studies in Philosophy and Education*, 28, 269–281.

Scholz, R. W. & Marks, D. (2004). Learning about transdisciplinarity: Where are we? Where have we been? Where should we go? In J. Thompson Klein, W. Grossenbacher-Mansuy, R. Häberli, A. Bill, R. W. Scholz, & M. Welti, M. (Eds.), *Transdisciplinarity: Joint problem solving among science, technology, and society. An effective way for managing complexity.* New York, NY: Springer.

Scribner, S. (1984). Literacy in three metaphors. *American Journal of Education*, 93(1), 6–21.

Shulman, L. S. (1986). Those who understand: Knowledge growth in teaching. *Educational Researcher*, 15(2), 4–14.

Siegel, M. (2006). Rereading the signs: Multimodal transformations in the field of literacy education. *Language Arts*, 84(1), 65–77.

Smith, N. B. (1896). *American reading instruction.* Newark, DE: International Reading Association.

Street, B. (2004). Futures of the ethnography of literacy? *Language and Education*, 18(4), 326–330.

The New London Group. (1996). A pedagogy of multiliteracies: Designing social futures. *Harvard Educational Review*, 66(1), 60–92.

Thompson Klein, J., Grossenbacher-Mansuy, W., Häberli, R., Bill, A., Scholz, R. W., & Welti, M. (Eds.), (2004). *Transdisciplinarity: Joint problem solving among science, technology, and society. An effective way for managing complexity.* New York, NY: Springer.

Torney-Purta, J. (2002). The school's role in developing civic engagement: A study of adolescents in twenty-eight countries. *Applied Developmental Science*, 6(4), 203–212.

Touraine, A. (1998). *What is democracy?* Boulder, CO: Westview Press.

Tierney, R. J. (2008). Learning with multiple literacies: Observations of lives exploring meanings, identities, possibilities, and worlds. In J. Flood, S. B. Heath, & D. Lapp (Eds.), *Handbook of research on teaching literacy through the communicative and visual arts* (Vol. II). New York, NY: Lawrence Erlbaum.

Tyson, C. A. (2003). A bridge over troubled water: Social studies, civic education, and critical race theory. In G. Ladson-Billings (Ed.), *Critical race theory: Perspectives on social studies* (pp. 15–25). Greenwich, CT: Information Age Publishing.

Tyson, C. & Park, S. C. (2008). Civic education, social justice, and critical race theory. In J. Arthur, I. Davies, & C. Hahn (Eds.), *The SAGE handbook of education for citizenship and democracy* (pp. 29–39). Thousand Oaks, CA: SAGE Publications.

VanFossen, P. J. (2005). "Reading and math take so much of the time . . . ": An overview of social studies instruction in elementary classrooms in Indiana. *Theory and Research in Social Education*, 33(3), 376–403.

Vogler, K. E. & Virtue, D. (2007). "Just the facts, ma'am": Teaching social studies in the era of standards and high-stakes testing. *Social Studies*, 98(2), 54–58.

Weiss, A. R., Lutkus, A. D., Grigg, W. S., & Niemi, R. G. (2001). The next generation of citizens: NAEP civics assessments: 1988 and 1998. *Education Statistics Quarterly*, 3(3), 21–24.

Westheimer, J. & Kahne, J. (2004). What kind of citizen? The politics of educating for democracy. *American Educational Research Journal*, 41(2), 237–269.

Wills, J. (2007). Putting the squeeze on social studies: Managing teaching dilemmas in subject areas excluded from state testing. *Teachers College Record*, 109(8), 1980–2046.

Young, I. M. (1990). *Justice and the politics of difference*. Princeton, NJ: Princeton University Press.

PART II
Teaching Critical Democratic Literacy

3

WHAT CAN I DO TO BE A GOOD CITIZEN?

A Kindergarten Unit on Civic Virtue

> *I raise up my voice—not so I can shout but so that those without a voice can be heard . . . we cannot succeed when half of us are held back.*
>
> — Malala Yousafzai

Background Content for Teachers

Civic Concept: Civic Virtue

In its most simple form, civic virtue is one's personal qualities necessary to live life as a good citizen for one's own benefit, and, just as importantly, the good of the community (Dagger, 1997; Galston, 2007; Merry, 2012). These qualities may be expressed as a disposition to behave in certain ways that are beneficial to the community and that protect the individual rights of all of the community's members. This means that sometimes a person might walk door-to-door to support a school bond because she believes the extra funds will help her community's children become better educated, bettering the entire community. She will do this knowing that she has no children in school and she will have to pay more in taxes. While the common or public good is clear in this display of civic virtue, the protection of individual rights may be less clear. But, this virtuous citizen believes that a very good way to protect everyone's individual rights is for all citizens, young and old, to be educated. Civic virtue is most often associated with a political philosophy called civic republicanism. Prioritizing the community, or common good, over one's personal interests is an essential understanding in civic virtue. However, it does not mean that individual rights do not matter. Instead, this particular philosophy asserts that the best way to protect individual rights is to protect the public good. For our very young citizens, this could mean listening carefully to what they need to do during a fire drill so that they can protect their own lives, as well as the lives of those around them. This may not seem overtly civic, but following rules that benefit the community and institutional safety are civic issues. Explicitly connecting this behavior to civic virtue will help students learn a civic vocabulary and begin to recognize that they have a civic life, even when they are too young to vote or run for office. Further, introducing civic virtue in this way to young students is consistent with a common social studies scope and sequence that focuses on the self in early elementary grades. But, we should go beyond the immediate and familiar in order to build conceptual understanding. In this chapter, civic virtue is introduced to kindergartners through the use of both historical and current examples. For a more thorough discussion of civic virtue, see Chapter 7.

Historical Content: Educational Access for All

Jane Addams, the first woman awarded the Nobel Peace Prize, was dedicated to improving her community. Her establishment of Hull House in Chicago demonstrated her adherence to civic virtue in her creation of what we know today as the field of social work. Hull House was one of the best-known settlement houses in the United States, although there were more than 400 settlement houses around the nation in the late nineteenth century and into the early twentieth century. The primary purpose of settlement houses was to alleviate the growing poverty of urban workers and their families in large industrial cities. During this time, the United States was experiencing rapid industrialization with the growth of railroads, the steel industry, and the growth of various types of factories, most of which were located in larger cities. Many Americans moved from rural areas to these cities looking for economic opportunity. In addition, many new immigrants were coming to the United States also looking for economic opportunities, as well as political safety. Hull House, co-created with Addams's friend Ellen Starr, had a homeless shelter and a daycare center, and offered classes to help new immigrants learn English and better understand the dominant American culture. In the late nineteenth and early twentieth centuries, Addams was also a political advocate for women as she played a leading role in the women's suffrage movement, worked on women's and children's health, and promoted world peace. She worked tirelessly in her own community of Chicago, including serving locally on the board of education, as well as nationally as chair of the Women's Peace Party, and internationally as president of the Women's International League for Peace and Freedom. Addams's lifetime of work is seen as seminal to education, health, and philosophy while at the same time it clearly demonstrates how one person can engage civically in the local and global communities to improve the lives of others.

In 2012, 15-year-old Malala Yousafzai, along with two school colleagues, was shot while riding a bus home from school in her hometown of Mingora, Pakistan. Specifically targeted by the Taliban because she advocated educating girls, Malala received death threats yet still attended school. Malala began her civic work at the age of 11 by blogging under a pseudonym about living under Taliban rule in Afghanistan as a female. She eventually became the subject of a documentary and a spokeswoman for education, actions which led to her being specifically targeted by the Taliban. After the assassination attempt, Malala was taken out of Afghanistan for advanced medical treatment, and after a long recovery from her severe wounds, Malala continues her commitment to speaking out for educational access for all girls. More recently she has advocated for the young women kidnapped by Boko Haram in Nigeria. Malala's tireless focus on education for all girls is connected to the civic virtue notion of solidarity.

Critical Democratic Literacy and Civic Virtue

Critical Democratic Literacy (CDL) frames civic virtue as the cornerstone of educating young students for civic life. In relation to CDL, civic virtue underlies the basic ideal of what beliefs and dispositions are necessary to participate in civic life and contribute to the good of one's community. While understanding that civic virtue is complex, it is integral to comprehending the responsibility of engaging in civic life beyond the self.

Rationale for the Unit <u>Sense of self & community</u>

Elementary students need a foundational understanding of civic virtue as they begin their civic education. Civic virtue provides a base from which to work for students by laying out the relationship, particularly responsibilities, between the self and the broader community, whether that be the classroom community, the global community, or something in between. By understanding that relationship, young learners can begin to see how they are members of a community, and that membership requires that they contribute to the common good. Many social studies curricular materials approach these ideas by relying on learning about the self and then moving on to neighborhoods, and then to larger community constructions such as cities, states, the nation, etc. This is often done by just looking at what the student can do in his or her community to have civic virtue or by looking at others around them who have civic virtue. This could include studying how the people who work in the school or people in the community like the mayor, police, fire personnel, etc., all contribute in positive ways. For our purposes we add to those ideas by situating the introduction to civic virtue within a historical context and by centering the instruction on the very concept of civic virtue. This approach requires teaching civic virtue conceptually in order to allow students to apply the concept as they learn how individuals enact civic virtue, and how in later lessons, civic virtue is connected to the other civic concepts (i.e., civic engagement, civil discourse, and civil disobedience).

Chapter Guide

The chapter moves through planning an entire unit on civic virtue for a kindergarten classroom. The concept of civic virtue and the activities presented could be adapted for other grade levels. See Chapter 7 for additional information. Table 3.1 provides an overview of the unit components and the basic areas addressed across the unit. Both theory and practice are combined in order to (1) incorporate the theoretical framework of CDL, (2) represent the construction and teaching of lessons focused on social studies and literacy standards, and (3) meet the needs of elementary learners. Table 3.1 begins with civic virtue as the social studies concept to be taught and then moves to an initial assessment before more specific lessons are designed. The assessment component focuses on both students and materials in order to adjust instruction based on teaching the students how to prioritize information. The unit is recursive and slowly builds up several areas in order to integrate them into the large concept of civic virtue. Beginning with identifying important elements of events using *The Important Book* (Brown, 1999), and moving to the specific stories of Malala Yousafzai and Jane Addams, the unit introduces basic ideas such as decision-making and then revisits them to build the deeper concept of civic virtue. Eventually, important decisions become good or bad decisions as they connect to helping others in the spirit of civic virtue. The typical social studies content for kindergarten is understanding the self in the context of broader communities, including the family and classroom communities. We use Addams and Malala to connect their lives to the lives of the students by focusing on what they could all share—essential elements of the concept of civic virtue. We also teach about Addams because she started a kindergarten at Hull House and the students are in kindergarten. We chose Malala because she is a student in school, just like the kindergarteners. Both of these points create a very concrete connection between the students and women under study. Addams's and Malala's demonstration of civic virtue within their communities is something that students should be able to relate to. The important things a person does soon become encased in what important decisions a particular person made. Finally, helping others by making good decisions becomes an aspect of civic virtue. While kindergarteners will have a simplistic understanding of civic virtue, they will have a means of describing and evaluating decisions made by themselves and others based on the principles of civic virtue. Table 3.1 provides an overview of the main components of the unit.

TABLE 3.1 Process guide for planning a unit on civic virtue

Civic Virtue			
Social Studies	Critical Literacy		
Self	Focusing on sociopolitical issues Taking action and promoting social justice		
⬇ *Initial Assessment*			
Students			
What do students know about the ideas of individual and community? What do students know about civic virtue (e.g., character, courage, justice, integrity)?	What do students know about comparing and contrasting multiple events/viewpoints? What do students know about social justice as it relates to individuals and communities (fairness)?		
Materials			
Videos: Jane Addams documentary videos Malala Yousafzai videos of appearances/speeches	Informational Text: *Malala Yousafzai: Warrior with Words* *Jane Addams: Pioneer Social Worker* Conceptual Text: *The Important Book*		
⬇ *Standards*			
Social Studies Standards (C3 Framework)	Literacy Speaking & Listening Standards (CCSS ELA)	Literacy Reading Standards (CCSS ELA)	Literacy Writing Standards (CCSS ELA)
Civic and Political Institutions: D2.Civ.2.K-2 Explain how all people, not just official leaders, play important roles in a community.	**Comprehension and Collaboration:** CCSS.ELA-Literacy.SL.K.1 Participate in collaborative conversations with diverse partners about *kindergarten topics and texts* with peers and adults in small and larger groups.	**Key Ideas and Details:** CCSS.ELA-Literacy.RI.K.2 With prompting and support, identify the main topic and retell key details of a text. CCSS.ELA-Literacy.RI.K.3 With prompting and support, describe the connection between two individuals, events, ideas, or pieces of information in a text.	**Text Types and Purposes:** CCSS.ELA-Literacy.W.K.3 Use a combination of drawing, dictating, and writing to narrate a single event or several loosely linked events, tell about the events in the order in which they occurred, and provide a reaction to what happened.

(*Continued*)

TABLE 3.1 Process guide for planning a unit on civic virtue (*Continued*)

Participation and Deliberation: Applying Civic Virtues and Democratic Principles: D2.Civ.7.K-2 Apply civic virtues when participating in school settings.	CCSS.ELA-Literacy. SL.K.2 Confirm understanding of a text read aloud or information presented orally or through other media by asking and answering questions about key details and requesting clarification if something is not understood.	Integration of Knowledge and Ideas: CCSS.ELA-Literacy. RI.K.7 With prompting and support, describe the relationship between illustrations and the text in which they appear (e.g., what person, place, thing, or idea in the text an illustration depicts).	Production and Distribution of Writing: CCSS.ELA-Literacy.W.K.6 With guidance and support from adults, explore a variety of digital tools to produce and publish writing, including in collaboration with peers.
Processes, Rules, and Laws: D2.Civ. 14.K-2 Describe how people have tried to improve their communities over time.	**Presentation of Knowledge and Ideas:** CCSS.ELA-Literacy.SL.K.4 Describe familiar people, places, things, and events and, with prompting and support, provide additional detail. CCSS.ELA-Literacy.SL.K.5 Add drawings or other visual displays to descriptions as desired to provide additional detail.	CCSS.ELA-Literacy. RI.K.9 With prompting and support, identify basic similarities in and differences between two texts on the same topic (e.g., in illustrations, descriptions, or procedures).	**Research to Build and Present Knowledge:** CCSS.ELA-Literacy.W.K.8 With guidance and support from adults, recall information from experiences or gather information from provided sources to answer a question.

Learning Objectives
Students will:

Social Studies	Critical Literacy
• Explain how each member of a community has a responsibility to the community. • Describe how leaders can do good things for themselves and others. • Determine how they can help others.	• Listen, discuss, and draw key details from individuals' lives and events. • Describe how Malala Yousafzai and Jane Addams took action to promote social justice for themselves and others.

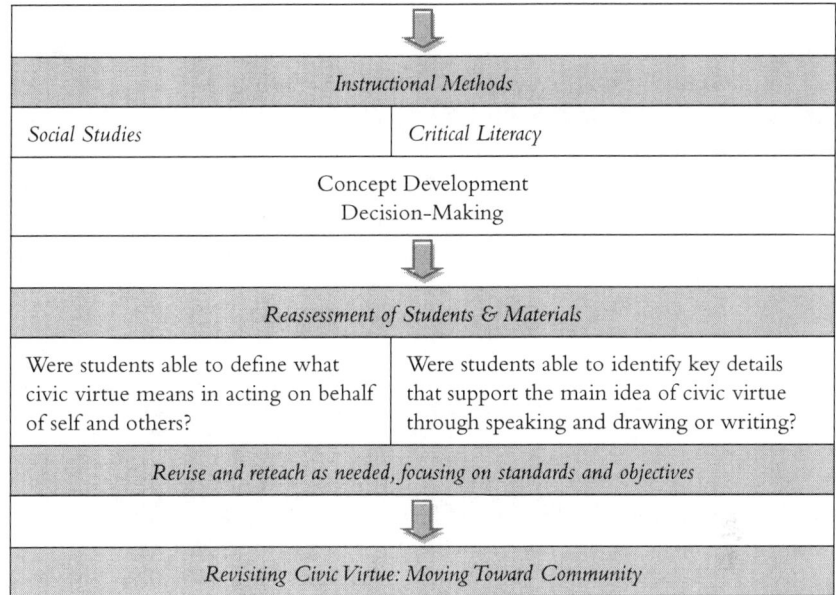

Unit Narrative

This chapter relies on the kindergarten classroom of Mr. Baxter. Mr. Baxter has been a kindergarten teacher for 12 years and taught in the same urban school in the Southwest during that time. He has 25 students in his classroom who speak a variety of languages and come from a broad range of socioeconomic backgrounds. Kindergarteners are typically emergent readers and writers. Emergent readers and writers are just beginning to recognize the conventions of print. As they begin to read, they rely heavily on pictures, oral language patterns they are familiar with, and memory. Their writing depends on invented spelling, where they can be seen spelling words using the sounds they hear (e.g., *dog* may be spelled as *dg*). With teacher support they can read and write texts and use their well-developed listening and speaking skills to understand concepts and ideas far beyond what they can read and write on their own.

Civic Virtue: Preparing the Lesson

Presenting a complex concept such as civic virtue to kindergarteners requires starting with a high interest and relatable example. Malala Yousafzai is a young girl who goes to school. Kindergartners can relate to that due to their daily experiences of going to school. Because concepts such as civic virtue by their nature are abstract, rather than beginning with Jane Addams, an adult who lived in an unfamiliar historical time period, Mr. Baxter starts with a current and young civic leader, Malala. Once students develop an understanding of Malala's life and work, he can initiate the conceptual learning of civic virtue across the exemplars of both Addams and Malala. Mr. Baxter is planning the unit at the beginning of the year so he can incorporate the other three civic concepts (civic engagement, civil discourse, and civil disobedience) later in his school year. Addressing civic virtue first allows him to not only establish a foundation for the additional areas, but it will also assist him in formulating classroom rules and a classroom climate where students understand the roles they have in the classroom community. He wants the students to be involved in establishing rules; however, he wants them to come to that discussion having studied civic virtue and having thought about what they could do that would be virtuous in civic life. Translating civic virtue into a comprehendible concept for 5- and 6-year-olds is dependent on Mr. Baxter's deep understanding of civic virtue as well as child development and emergent reading and writing levels, since many kindergarteners are beginning to read and write, and rely on pictures, discussion, and modeling in their learning. Civic virtue for kindergarteners should be as concrete as possible yet still abstract enough to translate across many examples in different times and different places in order to be retained and applied as a concept by the students. Kindergarten students can understand concepts such as good versus bad, fair versus unfair, etc. Previous readings and experiences, such as reading and discussing superheroes, will be used to set up the idea of people who do good things for others in situations that may be unfair or bad. This basic understanding will lay the groundwork for civic virtue for the kindergarteners. By starting with Malala, Mr. Baxter is drawing on their interest in other students, and they will be able to connect their identities as students to hers. He decides to begin by reading *The Important Book* to set up a framework for students to use as they listen to both Malala's and Addams's stories. In sharing the stories of both women, Mr. Baxter will ask the students to identify commonalities between them orally as he models writing using various charts.

Initial Assessment [most important thing]

Mr. Baxter brings the students together on the carpet as he reads *The Important Book* aloud. He periodically stops reading to ask students about the objects described in the book. Each object is presented and its attributes described with an emphasis on the most important thing (e.g., the most important thing about grass is that it is green). This reinforces the idea of both understanding the attributes of something and evaluating the most important attribute. Mr. Baxter leads the students in a discussion about the important things in their lives. He draws on students' ideas and builds up their ability to name attributes and evaluate them. Over the rest of the week, Mr. Baxter incorporates the idea of "the most important thing" into daily activities and objects. He realizes that kindergarteners need multiple exposures to concepts that they have direct experience with so that they can develop a deeper understanding. Mr. Baxter connects students' backpacks to the ideas in *The Important Book*. The students name attributes about their backpacks (they hold their snacks, they hold their crayons, they are blue, they are heavy). Then Mr. Baxter asks the students what the most important thing about their backpack is. After much discussion they determine that the most important thing about their backpack is that it carries all of their supplies for school. The discussion helps the kindergarteners learn to prioritize and debate attributes. They decided that the color of their backpacks is an attribute, but it was not the most important attribute of the backpacks. This crucial step in setting up the lesson allows Mr. Baxter to determine how his kindergarteners are able to process information and evaluate very familiar information. He needs to know if they are able to evaluate their backpacks, an item they use daily for school, before he can move onto the more abstract concept of civic virtue. Now that the class has worked through one example, Mr. Baxter continues the lesson throughout the rest of the week informally, and finally pulls the students together to address the task and reevaluate their understanding. On the way to the cafeteria, he asks students to watch for things they see in the cafeteria. As he picks them up from lunch he asks them what they saw in the cafeteria, what they know about recess, and what they know about movie characters such as Superman. Luis raises his hand to state that, "Superman saves people," and Carla shares, "The cafeteria was really loud today and Elisa got in trouble; she dropped her food . . ." Mr. Baxter nods and says, "Is the cafeteria 'loud'?" The students nod as he turns to write "is loud" on the chart. He continues, "What else can we say that the cafeteria has?" He listens carefully and guides their discussion as he records their contributions on a chart (see Table 3.2).

TABLE 3.2 The most important thing

Person/Place/Thing	Things About the Person/Place/Thing	Most Important Thing About the Person/Place/Thing
Cafeteria	Has dishes Smells good Makes food Is loud	Makes food
Recess	You can see your friends Has swings Is loud	See friends
Superman	Flies Saves people Is strong	Saves people

The students continue this type of analysis of people, places, and things throughout the week and add to their chart. In relation to literacy, the students are learning to use their listening and speaking skills to participate in collaborative conversations; learning to describe familiar people, places, things, and events; and they are learning a foundational skill (parts of speech) as they complete the chart. Once it is clear that the students understand how to identify details based on their own knowledge and then decide on the most important aspect of their selected topic, Mr. Baxter moves to introducing Malala and her life to the students. Having some background knowledge about Malala, Mr. Baxter knew that she had been specifically targeted and shot in the head by the Taliban. Keeping this knowledge in mind, as well as the age of his students, he knew he would have to address this carefully. He decided that telling his students specifically that Malala had been shot in the head was not appropriate. However, he knew that the assassination attempt was an important part of her story; it was addressed in the websites and children's literature he reviewed, and his students needed some aspect of this information in order to understand the concept of civic virtue in Malala's life. Mr. Baxter decided that for his very young students, most of whom who could not read, he could introduce this information by telling his students that, "Malala was hurt badly by some people who did not want her to go to school and wanted her to stop talking about girls going to school." He introduces the children's book, *Malala Yousafzai: Warrior with Words* (Abouraya, 2014) and begins a read-aloud concentrated on simply sharing Malala's story. The students are engaged in the plot and his questions highlight the sequence of events on this first reading. He asks them what happened first, etc. Mr. Baxter draws students' attention to her chronological story. He stops periodically to ask questions aligned with each event as described in the story. He creates a simple story map with the students listing what happens at the beginning of the story, in the middle, and at the end. Guiding their story comprehension allows him to hone in on the overall story of Malala going to school, being told not to go to school, then being hurt for going to school, and finally returning to school. This attention to the literacy skills of sequencing and identifying the main idea is a goal of reading instruction, and it provides the students with a concrete conception of what Malala did before civic virtue is introduced conceptually. It also provides Mr. Baxter with an initial assessment of students' ability to listen to and comprehend a text.

As Mr. Baxter completes the second reading of the book the next day, he asks students what they noticed about Malala. Students share that she was a girl, that she lived far away, and that she had friends. Some students mention her not being able to attend school. Bringing the topic back to the most important thing, Mr. Baxter adjusts *The Most Important Thing* chart to now focus just on people (Table 3.3), asking students to return to their tables to draw their ideas about Malala on small 6 x 6 inch squares of paper. Attempting to redirect their attention from her personal appearance and life, he asks the students to think about

TABLE 3.3 The most important thing: Focus on a person

Person	Things About the Person	The Most Important Thing About the Person
Malala Yousafzai	Read books Went to school Has friends Got hurt	

the things that Malala did. Mr. Baxter reminds students that Malala did a lot of things in the book and focuses their attention on drawing her activities. Due to kindergarteners' emerging literacy skills, he makes sure they have time to prewrite and use their drawing skills to convey their understandings. He puts the students in groups of three at tables so they can discuss their ideas. Listening and speaking skills are crucial as part of the comprehension and writing process.

As the students draw and retell the story and share their ideas with peers at their tables, Mr. Baxter circulates around the room. He observes and asks students questions about their choices. This includes questions about why they chose Malala going to school, spending time with her friends, and getting hurt as the most important things. Then they all convene on the carpet and students present their drawings to the group. Most of the students have copied the illustrations in the book and have some sense of the basic ideas in her story. This author's chair activity allows not only for students' comprehension reinforcement, but also it is another opportunity for Mr. Baxter to assess their understanding and their writing. Emergent writers will rely on drawings, but as they progress they will use labeling and invented spelling. Mr. Baxter notes that some students drew Malala, her school bus, and her sitting at school, and some students were able to draw and add her name and some text. Mr. Baxter posts and labels each student's drawing and writing onto the chart.

CRITICAL DEMOCRATIC LITERACY

CDL requires that citizens are thoroughly informed about issues and can think critically about them, even when the facts about the issues are disturbing or difficult. Facilitating effective discussion and educative experiences about difficult issues in the elementary curriculum can help to equip students to work through similar issues in their personal and public lives (Ballantine & Hill, 2000; McBee, 1996).

The next day, Mr. Baxter shows a short video clip of Malala being interviewed about finally going to school. He also shows a clip of her speaking to the United Nations about girls' education. Before and after each brief clip he discusses Malala's work today. He tells the students about her speaking tours and her books, her meetings with political figures, and her website. After the video clips and discussion, he rereads specific sections of the Malala children's book and introduces the idea of civic virtue by asking students what the most important thing was about Malala's decision to go to school. Several students mention her desire to learn while others highlight her wanting to be with her friends. Mr. Baxter asks the students about Malala going to school in order to help her friends. During a long discussion about the importance of helping friends, the kindergartners demonstrate various examples in their own lives of how they have helped people they know, such as their families or friends. Jesse and Liliya both provide examples of how they help their moms at home by setting the table for dinner and picking up their toys. Mr. Baxter redirects the discussion by asking, "How is Malala helping other people?" Jill says, "She told lots of people that girls should go to school," and Damien offers, "She started a group on the Internet for girls." Mr. Baxter realizes that the students have a simplistic understanding of civic virtue, still strongly connected to Malala and her friends. As kindergartners, their experiences differ, yet they do understand the basic notion that Malala acted not only on her behalf, but also on the behalf of her peers, a concept of solidarity and honor that is integral to conceptions of civic virtue. His lessons will now turn to bringing the standards into the formal lesson on civic virtue.

Standards

Mr. Baxter's unit on civic virtue focuses on three standards from the Disciplinary Concepts and Tools section of the C3 Framework (NCSS, 2013). Specifically, Mr. Baxter focuses on three civics standards that incorporate both self and community. This fits with his intent to help the students see themselves as active citizens who can help themselves and do good for others. While most of the Common Core State Standards for English/Language Arts (CCSS ELA) could apply to the unit, Mr. Baxter elects to hone in on several related to speaking, listening, reading, and writing. Understanding that kindergartners are developing their reading and writing skills through opportunities for listening and discussion, Mr. Baxter selected principles focused on integrating all four modes of literacy into the lessons.

Learning Objectives: "What Can I do to Be a Good Citizen?"

Bringing civic virtue alive for kindergartners, Mr. Baxter utilizes the social studies concept of leaders to connect individuals from today to those from history who have exhibited civic virtue. Mr. Baxter introduces the concept of leader by

TABLE 3.4 Learning objectives

Students will:	
Social Studies	*Critical Literacy*
• Explain how each member of a community has a responsibility to the community. • Describe how leaders can do good things for themselves and others. • Determine how they can help others.	• Listen, discuss, and draw key details from individuals' lives and events. • Describe how Malala Yousafzai and Jane Addams took action to promote social justice for themselves and others.

connecting it to the more familiar concepts of hero and heroine. Relying on stories and biographies of the lives of heroes, heroines, and leaders gives students real world examples of civic virtue as it was enacted by real people.

Table 3.4 provides a reminder of Mr. Baxter's social studies and literacy objectives. The objectives are closely related, a testament to the ease with which social studies and literacy can be integrated. The critical literacy objectives are related to both the four tenets of critical literacy (depicted in Chapter 8) and the kindergarten CCSS ELA.

Instructional Methods

Bringing civic virtue into the concepts of heroines and leaders who make decisions for themselves and others is the focus of the following lessons. Integrating social studies and literacy methods, Mr. Baxter designs a lesson on the concept of civic virtue and then follows up with adding in historical content by using the story of Jane Addams. Relying on the question, "What can I do to be a good citizen?" (i.e., someone who displays civic virtue), he begins with a concept development (Taba, 1967) lesson on civic virtue.

Concept Development Lesson

Concepts are sometimes called big ideas or generalizations, and their abstractness makes concepts difficult to learn, especially for young students. They are usually just one word, like *justice*, or two words, like *civic virtue*. Social studies is full of concepts, including democracy, map, interdependence, religion, perspective, change, frontier, and social movement, among others. The 10 strands of the National Council for the Social Studies Curriculum Standards (2010) are also concepts. They are abstract with numerous concrete examples, and often interdisciplinary. We can often think of examples of a concept, but defining the concept is much harder. Think about the concept of war. It might be easy to come up with examples like the Revolutionary War, the Civil War, the Spanish American

War, World War I, the War on Poverty, the War on Drugs, and the War on Terror, but what do they all share? Misconceptions typically occur when people take one or two examples of a concept and use that as a definition. If we use the Spanish American War and World War I to guide our definition, we assume that a war includes at least two nations engaged in military conflict. That works for those two examples, but it does not work for the US Civil War because it was a military conflict between two sides within one country. It also does not work for the War on Poverty—that was an organized political agenda designed to fight the causes of cyclical poverty, and did not involve the military at all. Instead, we build our understanding or definition of a concept by using numerous examples in order to identify the essential elements or criterial attributes (Taba, 1967) of the concept. These elements or attributes are the ones that *all* examples of the concept must have. We also identify those elements that are not essential (non-criterial attributes) because only *some* of the examples have them. If we go back to the example of war and look at our examples, we can tell that *all* of our examples include some type of organized conflict—that is an essential element or criterial attribute. We can also determine that involving the military in battles is a non-essential or non-criterial attribute because only *some* wars include military battles. As students go through multiple examples, they discard the non-essential elements or non-criterial attributes because they are not necessary to understand and define the concept. By going through this process, we begin to build the definition—wars include organized conflicts of some type. What we have done in this process is to begin with facts (i.e., examples of wars) and use those facts to build generalizations, or the concept of war. This is an important point—facts are used to build larger understandings; facts are not learned in isolation or as the end goal.

In the civic virtue lessons, we use the concept development strategy of list, group, label: attributes are listed, put into similar groups and given a descriptive label. Older students who have had prior experience may come up with their own groupings and labels. However, for younger elementary students, including those in our lessons, the teacher predetermines the groupings and labels. That is, the teacher predetermines the essential elements or criterial attributes of the concept, and the students decide what they should list (revisit Table 3.3). Mr. Baxter is beginning to build his students' conceptual understanding of civic virtue in a modified list, group, label process. The middle column has a list of things about Malala that the students recalled from the story (non-essential or non-criterial) and the third column has the students list the most important thing about Malala (essential or criterial). Mr. Baxter is not creating Malala as a concept; rather, the students are identifying characteristics of Malala's civic virtue. As Mr. Baxter continues the lesson, the students continue to build their conceptual understanding of civic virtue by learning about civic heroes and heroines like Malala, Jane Addams, and others. They list essential elements of civic virtue for each of these people. Mr. Baxter has the goal of having students understand civic virtue as the inclination and ability for someone to stand up for his or her rights as well as the rights of others—this is his definition of civic virtue. As he continues, he designs follow-up lessons using multiple modes of instruction. Mr. Baxter then returns to Malala's story by showing a brief video of her speech to the United Nations. In the speech she discusses the importance of school and speaking up for those who cannot speak for themselves. Stopping the video at several points, Mr. Baxter stresses how Malala framed her experiences in what was going on in her community and how she realized that her actions helped everyone in the community. She used all of what happened to her, including the attempted assassination, to continue to speak out and lead with a larger civic purpose in mind, going beyond her community to advocating for girls' education everywhere in the world. The underlying use of heroes and heroines to support civic virtue is connected to the unit through the use of a writing and dramatic play center to encourage oral language development and reiterate the connections between civic leaders acting for the benefit of all and the actions of superheroes.

In order to move beyond simply understanding Malala and her life, it is crucial that the students can apply the concept of civic virtue to other situations and contexts. After a review of Malala's story and the chart detailing her most important civic act, continuing to attend and speak out for the right for everyone to attend school, Mr. Baxter introduces the story of Addams. To build interest and background knowledge for the kindergarteners, he shows a short video of Hull House and how she began a kindergarten for young children in Chicago. The video is full of images showing Addams with young children doing activities related to school and families at Hull House. The images depict contexts that are familiar to the kindergarteners: they too go to school, sit on the floor and listen to their teacher, and see family members at their school building. Mr. Baxter stops the video several times to point out these connections to the kindergarteners. He asks them to notice how the pictures compare to their school. The students notice that the pictures are all black and white, that the people are wearing funny clothes, but they also notice that they are reading books and talking to each other. Mr. Baxter mentions that the last two things, reading and talking in school, are the most important things about Addams.

To add more detailed information about Addams, he reads a short biography about her life and discusses her works and legacy with the students. As he reads, he shares additional images of Addams and Hull House. The images, many of which were found on the Swarthmore College website, displayed on the interactive whiteboard, focus on her efforts working with children in the Hull House kindergarten. Mr. Baxter explains how the kindergarten was part of her work in her community. He tells the students that both Addams and Malala won a Nobel Peace Prize for all of the work they did for others and for world peace. Mr. Baxter tells the students about the prize and how it is given to people who help other people. The concept of civic virtue is connected to working for the betterment of others. The kindergarteners need to begin to see how both women were in service to their respective communities. Another aspect of civic virtue that

TABLE 3.5 The most important thing: Focus on a person

Person	Things About the Person	The Most Important Thing About the Person
Malala Yousafzai	Read books Went to school Helped girls go to school	Helped girls go to school
Jane Addams	Opened a house to help people Helped kids go to kindergarten Won a prize	Helped kids go to kindergarten

Mr. Baxter is aware of is the conscious movement of both women to enact civic virtue. They both purposefully made decisions, some with great risk and consequences, to help others. Therefore, Mr. Baxter knows he has to connect Malala's story to Addams's life through the skill of decision-making. Mr. Baxter begins this process by guiding the students back to the *The Most Important Thing* chart (Table 3.5). He asks the students what they should add about Addams. As the students share their ideas, he records them, modeling writing, spelling, and reinforcing the skills of evaluation and comprehension.

With guidance, the students connect both Malala and Addams to how they both worked for children who needed schools. Mr. Baxter emphasizes how both civic leaders saw education as a way to help people and how they both wanted everyone to have an education. He asks the students why they go to school, how school can help them when they grow up, and what would happen if they did not go to school.

Heroes and Heroines Center

The story of Malala can be far removed from students' experiences and Jane Addams is very distant in time for some students. Mr. Baxter realizes the need to bring in additional materials to continue to develop the concept of civic virtue. One of his centers is set up in as a writing center next to a dramatic play area. The writing center consists of comic books and simple stories and pictures of comic book heroes and heroines such as Superman and Wonder Woman. By accessing the already familiar concepts of heroes and heroines, Mr. Baxter will use the characteristics that heroes and heroines have (e.g., courage, bravery) to connect to the less familiar and new concept of civic virtue, as many characteristics are similar. These similar characteristics are the ones that Mr. Baxter highlights. Costumes are set up in the play area for students as they use dramatic play in the classroom and during recess time. Students are encouraged to retell and reenact stories from the unit and draw and write their retellings. The dramatic play is prompted to connect to the notion of what a hero is, and students are required to draw or write a story about a hero of their choice to be shared by the end of the week. Previous read-alouds and discussions by the students in informal settings such as recess and lunch indicate that they have some familiarity with superheroes due to popular movies. Mr. Baxter decides to build on this prior knowledge by bringing in Superman to again adjust the chart, providing a new title reflecting the concepts under study: heroes/heroines and civic virtue (Table 3.6). He also adjusts two column titles, reflecting what they did for themselves and the actions they took to help others.

As he made these adjustments, he explained that Malala and Addams could be seen as heroines because of their courage and the good things that they did. Mr. Baxter builds on earlier work on identifying the most important thing, but now turns specifically to developing civic virtue. He highlights how the people in the chart identified an issue or problem they saw and then made a decision about the most important thing they could do about it. He again adjusts the chart (Table 3.6), adding the word *decision* to the right column, and asks the students how the decisions were made. He leads the students into understanding that all of the people they have read about had considered different options about what they could do to help other people. Mr. Baxter helped the students think about other reasonable options that were available (e.g., Malala could write her blog, but maybe not give speeches). He then adds in the idea of civic virtue and explicitly introduces the vocabulary words to the kindergarteners. For 5- and 6-year-olds, ideas about good and bad represent a clear dichotomy. There is little gray area. Fairy tales and many superhero stories clearly designate good and bad characters and good triumphs over evil. Building on this developmental understanding,

TABLE 3.6 Heroes and heroines of civic virtue

	Heroes and Heroines of CIVIC VIRTUE	
Person	*Things the person did for themselves*	*The most important ~~thing they did~~ decision they made for others*
Superman	Wrote stories for a newspaper	Got the bad guy
Malala Yousafzai	Read books Went to school Helped girls go to school	Helped girls go to school
Jane Addams	Opened a house to help people Helped kids go to kindergarten Won a prize	Helped kids go to kindergarten

Mr. Baxter draws the students' attention to all of the good things that Addams and Malala did for people. He emphasizes that they both made conscious decisions that made their communities better for others and connects this to the concept of civic virtue and its relationship to solidarity and engaging in the larger world. The chart also assists the students with not only describing two individuals and events, it guides them through the two women's stories so they can understand the basic similarities between the two stories (texts) on the same topic using illustrations and descriptions.

> **CRITICAL DEMOCRATIC LITERACY**
>
> Ideas such as establishing criteria, particularly criteria that emphasize citizens' responsibilities, considering alternatives, and using information to make thoughtful and informed decisions, are all key to developing CDL in young students.

Decision-Making

As the students discuss the virtuous acts of the people in their chart, Mr. Baxter hones in on the social studies' skill of decision-making. In teaching decision-making, students learn to weigh different options or alternatives based on criteria, carefully researching all of the feasible options. After thoughtful consideration of how each option meets each criterion, students choose the best alternative or option. Decision-making, often a part of economics, is connected to civic education in that people make informed decisions about how they engage in their daily lives. They decide what activities to do, where to go, and more specifically, who to vote for. In voting, people cannot vote for all of the candidates for mayor or president, they must choose the best among the available alternatives or options (i.e., candidates). When examining historical events, decision-making unpacks how and why people make conscious choices that affect the lives of others and subsequently alter history (Obenchain & Morris, 2015). Mr. Baxter realizes that his students already understand the basics of decision-making (e.g., "If someone takes my marker, I can hit them, tell the teacher, or I can use my words to ask for it back"), but he wants them to be able to see the process of decision-making as a social studies skill so they can apply the process to their own civic experiences.

Mr. Baxter begins by using Malala's story and creating a story template for students to use. His story template is based on identifying the options that Malala had regarding school. He gives each pair of students a sheet of construction paper with the template shown in Figure 3.1.

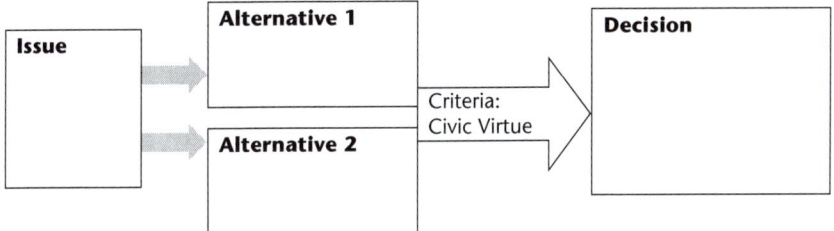

FIGURE 3.1 Malala's decision

He instructs the students to discuss an important part in Malala's story when she had to make a decision and to draw that part (e.g., Malala really wanted girls to go to school to learn, but was told by some people that girls could not go to school) in the first box. Mr. Baxter then reminds students that they need to think about two different decisions that Malala could have made to resolve that event or issue (e.g., Malala could stop going to school OR Malala could continue going to school). Once they have determined two reasonable alternatives, they should draw an illustration of each alternative in the two boxes in the middle section of the template. Then Mr. Baxter reintroduces a brief discussion about civic virtue. The students look back at the Heroes and Heroines of Civic Virtue (see Table 3.6) in which Malala, Jane Addams, and Superman made a decision to help themselves, and importantly, they also made a virtuous decision that helped others. Mr. Baxter then asks the students to talk about and draw their ideas about what decision Malala made that showed that she had civic virtue (e.g., Malala continued to go to school). Purposefully leaving the ideas to the students, this open-ended activity will allow him to evaluate not only what the students remember about the story but also how they put the sequence of events together, connecting it to decision-making. Mr. Baxter then leads the students in a discussion about why she decided to go to school and how her decision was based on her access to education but is also tied to all girls being able to go to school. Mr. Baxter accentuates the conscious decision or choice Malala made. He then goes back to the civic virtue chart to talk the students through how Addams made a decision to help others after she visited a settlement house. He asks students what types of decisions they, their parents, and other people they know make. It is important for students to understand that while Malala and Addams did amazing things for others, they, even as kindergarteners, can also make conscious decisions to help others. These collaborative conversations develop not only the kindergarteners' ability to listen and speak in a large group, they also develop the idea of how to relate information about two different people and connect their lives to each other, both CCSS ELA standards for the lesson. This attention to the lives of Malala and Addams attends to critical notions of how it was important for both women to disrupt the ideas present in their own communities of not providing education to

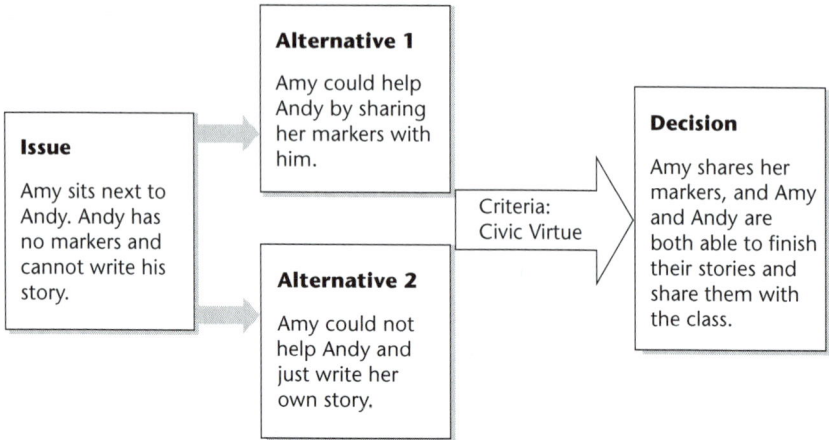

FIGURE 3.2 Amy's decision to share her markers using the criteria of civic virtue

all students, as well as the idea that individuals can take action to promote justice for all. These tenets of critical literacy are strongly connected to civic virtue due to their recognition that everyone is connected. Kindergarteners can see the relationship between helping someone else and making a thoughtful decision to do so. Mr. Baxters's students share how they might decide to help their neighbor rake leaves instead of playing a video game, or how they could help their family with chores instead of going to play. Mr. Baxter connects all of the students' points by creating a class template and calling it a decision-making guide. He takes some of the student connections, such as one student's decision to share her markers, and creates a visual process template (see Figure 3.2).

After several examples are shared, Mr. Baxter talks about making good decisions and how making civically virtuous decisions means that people make good decisions for themselves and for other people. The class then reviews some examples from the books and personal experiences. Kindergarten students need multiple exposures to ideas and very short mini-lessons. Further, developing conceptual understanding requires multiple opportunities to examine the concept and test the concept against new examples. As a result, these discussions occur over time and allow Mr. Baxter to incorporate the ideas about decision-making and civic virtue into all types of examples.

Evaluation

At the end of the unit, Mr. Baxter has several types of assessments to review. He has his observational notes, student group work, student center stories and drawings, and class discussions. He keeps the social studies and CCSS ELA standards as well as the conceptual definition of civic virtue in mind as he begins his assessment.

In order for him to assess individual students at the conclusion of the unit, he provides each student with drawing and writing materials and asks them to draw or write how people can help others by making good decisions. This activity allows students to use information from the books or their personal experiences to share their comprehension of the concept of civic virtue. Once students are done they participate in a whole group authors' chair reading of their drawing or writing. This provides Mr. Baxter with both a written and oral example of students' work. He comments and guides discussions of each student's example and ties their ideas back to Malala and Addams. He records their readings and explanations using anecdotal notes, attends to students who are still working toward understanding the concept of civic virtue, and follows up with them individually.

Reassessment of Students and Materials

After the author's chair sharing, Mr. Baxter notes that several students are confusing sharing with civic virtue. While sharing could be a type of civic virtue if it helps someone else, as it relates to Amy's example, civic virtue is more than sharing. He decides to return to Malala's work to focus on injustice and standing up for others' rights. To move away from just sharing Mr. Baxter decides to ask his students to go beyond their own classroom and participate in issues directly related to social justice. For kindergartners this simply means that the students should be able to see larger issues of injustice (unfairness) that relate to contexts beyond their own immediate world.

Revisiting Civic Virtue: Moving Toward Community

In order to move the concept of civic virtue into the real world for the students and hone in on justice, Mr. Baxter plans a culminating activity that engages the students outside of the classroom. He assists the students in deciding how they would like to raise funds to donate to the Malala Fund. He shows the students her website and shares a few more videos of her speaking to various interviewers about her call for education for all. Mr. Baxter delves deeper into the idea that in many parts of the world today girls are not allowed to attend school. He explains that yes, they learned about her bravery and now she can go to school, but he emphasizes that she had to go to another country to go to school. He explains how the Malala Fund supports education for girls in four countries—Pakistan, Nigeria, Jordan, and Kenya. Mr. Baxter sets up specific parameters for the students and then lets them choose how they would like to raise the funds. This is an opportunity for the students to participate in informed decision-making. One option is to have students participate in a service-learning project where they create greeting cards to celebrate Women's Day in early March and International Children's Day in early June. This provides a curricular connection as students utilize reading, writing, and drawing to design the cards. The students could sell the cards to others in the school and have a booth at the school's holiday bazaar. The proceeds would be donated to the Malala Fund. The second option is a much simpler approach and involves asking family and friends to donate their extra change. The students would collect the change in a large jar in the classroom, donating it whenever the change jar is filled. Both options are designed to let students play a role in making their own school a better place and assist students in another country. Keeping civic virtue in the forefront, the students also draw and write about their ideas and share them throughout the school by posting pictures and stories in the classroom and in the hallway. The goal is to engage the entire school and let the kindergarteners serve as educators by retelling the stories of Jane Addams and Malala Yousafzai to their peers. Concept development is key for students to transfer the concept to new events and situations; bringing civic virtue into various lessons maintains the concept across time. The unit on civic virtue continues throughout the rest of school year. Mr. Baxter relies on the concept as he covers other content areas and school events, and he ties it to his classroom rules. By giving students a clear initial understanding of civic virtue he realizes that he can use it to build on the other civic concepts.

Suggested Resources

There are several online resources available related to the unit. All of the sources were current as of the book's printing and may change over time. You are encouraged to expand on these and continue to seek out additional resources as you plan your unit.

Websites
Malala Yousafzai

> http://www.Malala.org
> http://www.globaleducationfirst.org/malaladay.html

Jane Addams

> http://www.uic.edu/jaddams/hull/_learn/_aboutjane/aboutjane.html
> http://ocp.hul.harvard.edu/ww/addams.html
> http://www.nobelprize.org/nobel_prizes/peace/laureates/1931/addams
>   -facts.html
> http://ocp.hul.harvard.edu/immigration/settlement.html
> http://www.swarthmore.edu/Library/peace/index.htm

Videos

ABC Special Digital Report (Malala's speech to the United Nations)
ABC video "Malala Returns to School"

References

Abouraya, K. L. (2014). *Malala Yousafzai: Warrior with words.* Great Neck, NY: StarWalk Kids Media.
Ballantine, D. & Hill, L. (2000). Teaching beyond "Once Upon a Time." *Language Arts,* 78(1), 11–20.
Brown, M. W. (1999). *The important book.* New York, NY: HarperCollins.
Dagger, R. (1997). *Civic virtues: Rights, citizenship, and republican liberalism.* Oxford, UK: Oxford University Press.
Galston, W. A. (2007). Pluralism and civic virtue. *Social Theory and Practice,* 33(4), 625–635.
McBee, R. H. (1996). Can controversial topics be taught in the early grades? The answer is yes! *Social Education,* 60(1), 38–41.
Obenchain, K. M. & Morris, R. V. (2015). *50 social studies strategies for K–8 classrooms.* Boston, MA: Pearson.
National Council for the Social Studies. (2010). *National curriculum standards for social studies: A framework for teaching, learning, and assessment.* Silver Spring, MD: Author.
National Council for the Social Studies (2013). *Social studies for the next generation: Purposes, practices, and implications of the college career, and civic life (C3) framework for social studies state standards.* Silver Spring, MD: Author.
Simon, C. (1998). *Jane Addams: Pioneer social worker.* Chicago, IL: Children's Press.
Stein, E. K. (2010). *Wonder Woman classic: I am Wonder Woman.* New York, NY: HarperCollins.
Taba, H. (1967). *Teacher's handbook for elementary social studies.* New York, NY: Addison-Wesley.
Wrecks, B. & Beavers, E. (2013). *Superman!* New York: Random House.

4

WHEN AND HOW SHOULD I GET INVOLVED IN CIVIC LIFE?

A Third-Grade Unit on Civic Engagement

Oh, if I could but live another century and see the fruition of all the work for women! There is so much yet to be done.

Susan B. Anthony

Background Content for Teachers

Civic Concept: Civic Engagement

Civic engagement is the individual or collective actions that people take to make their communities better. It requires action. This spans examples including one person's volunteerism at a local spay/neuter clinic to reduce pet overpopulation in the community, the youth uprising in Egypt that demanded an improved political and economic state, and the formal form of engagement—voting in political elections. An important and distinguishing part of this definition is the civic dimension that specifically addresses public issues and is for the benefit of the community. For example, volunteering for a neighborhood garage sale is community involvement and engagement, but it does not contain a civic or public dimension as it does not address public issues or policy concerns; it is not civic engagement. Democracy, as a political system that derives its power and direction from the people, requires its citizens to engage in the civic and political lives of their communities. Civic engagement is a way to convey to elected and appointed leaders what we believe is important and will make the community better for everyone. In other words, civic engagement is a civic responsibility. The necessity of citizen involvement is related to the idea of a *social contract*, first explored by Aristotle and later by political philosophers like Thomas Hobbes, John Locke, and Jean Jacque Rousseau. In sum, members of a community enter into a contract with one another to protect their basic or natural rights of life, liberty, and property. By doing so, people choose to give up some of their individual freedoms (e.g., yelling "FIRE!" in a crowded theater when there is no fire) in order to protect the rights of everyone (e.g., to not be trampled in the theater rushing to an exit). The main way that people in a community do this is by establishing a government that has as its major responsibility the protection of all of its citizens' natural rights. For our purposes, we connect civic engagement to exercising our rights and responsibilities. This allows elementary students to see that civic engagement is a citizen's responsibility to protect his or her rights, as well as the rights of others.

Historical Content: The Women's Rights Movement and Claiming the Right to Vote

The passage of the 19th Amendment to the US Constitution in 1920, extending the right to vote (i.e., suffrage) to female citizens is an important and well-known achievement in an ongoing women's rights movement (WRM). Those advocating women's rights have been civically engaged since before there was a United States. Abigail Adams's 1776 reminder to her husband, and eventual second US President, John Adams, to "remember the ladies" as he and other political leaders worked on the American colonies' Declaration of Independence from Great Britain is one early example. Mrs. Adams wanted her husband and the other founders to consider the protection of the natural rights of women while they were also considering how best to protect and advance the rights of white men. Unfortunately, the early founders chose to not specifically mention women or offer any civil rights to them in either the Declaration or in the 1787 US Constitution. Further, female citizens were not considered persons under law as their legal status was linked to their fathers and husbands. This meant that, in addition to being denied the right to vote, women had limited property ownership rights and were denied the right to pursue certain careers, access to higher education, equal pay, and divorce and child custody protection, among other denials.

The strongest push for women's rights began in the mid-nineteenth century with the organization of the Seneca Falls Convention on July 19 and 20, 1848, organized in large part by Elizabeth Cady Stanton and Lucretia Mott, along with three other women. Stanton and Mott, both abolitionists, first met in Europe while attending meetings focused on ending African American enslavement. Unfortunately, as women, their voices were not acknowledged. They reconnected in New York and decided to also specifically address women's rights.

They were not giving up their work to end enslavement; rather, they believed that without their own political rights as women, it was increasingly difficult to have any real power in their abolitionist work. Together, Stanton and Mott, along with Martha Wright, Mary Ann McClintock, and Jane Hunt, organized the Seneca Falls meetings. Approximately 100 people, mostly women, attended the convention in Seneca Falls, NY. The group pushed for civil rights broadly, including ending African American enslavement. Further, achieving suffrage for both women and African Americans was a specific goal. During this time, a lot of citizens worked together on expanding the rights of both groups. Frederick Douglass, a well-known African American abolitionist, also attended the convention and was one of the male signers of the Declaration of Sentiments, which detailed women's lack of civil rights and lack of protection from the government and was the most recognizable outcome of the convention. Elizabeth Cady Stanton was the primary author of the Declaration of Sentiments, which was modeled after the Declaration of Independence and stated that "all men and women are created equal" and listed the same number of grievances against the US government that the early founders had listed against the King of England. Two examples of grievances included in the Declaration of Sentiments are: "He has compelled her to submit to law in the formation of which she had no voice," and "He has made her, if married, in the eye of the law, civilly dead." For women, these grievances were evidence that the government was not enforcing the social contract that should protect women's natural rights, just as it should protect the rights of all citizens. As important as the Seneca Falls Convention was in uniting those interested in women's suffrage, the WRM faltered in part because of timing. A little more than a decade later, the United States was embroiled in a devastating Civil War that tore the country apart and women's rights were put aside. After the war and Reconstruction, and by the end of the nineteenth century, middle- and upper-class women became more civically engaged in a variety of public and policy issues including temperance (alcohol prohibition) and suffrage.

    A new generation of leaders was born, including Alice Paul and Lucy Burns, founders of the National Woman's Party, who carried the message of women's rights, including the right to vote, into the passage of the 19th Amendment in 1920. President Wilson, well known for his leadership during World War I, was initially opposed to women gaining the right to vote. Large numbers of women marched in Washington, DC; and dozens, known as silent sentinels, picketed for months in front of the White House. Women's rights advocates thought that it was hypocritical that President Wilson could lead the United States into World War I in order to preserve and protect democracy in Europe when US policies at home were not democratic. In particular, denying the right to vote to nearly one-half of its adult citizens (i.e., women) did not seem very democratic. Marchers and picketers were often attacked by onlookers, mostly male, while the police did nothing to protect the protesters. In addition, many protesters, including the silent sentinels, were arrested and jailed. Many of these protestors continued their protests in jail by going on hunger strikes. Officials reacted to these hunger strikes by force feeding many of the women. Ultimately, the political tide began to change as women's suffrage was adopted in several states (for local and state elections) and sympathy grew for the women protestors—wives, daughters, mothers, and grandmothers. President Wilson offered his support for the 19th Amendment and it passed both houses of Congress in 1919. It took another year, sustained advocacy, and a continued push in the states for the required two-thirds of the states to ratify the amendment. Female citizens over the age of 21 were finally allowed to vote in federal elections when Tennessee became the 36th state to ratify the 19th Amendment in August 1920. It is important to remember that the WRM continues. The Equal Rights Amendment to the US Constitution, passed by Congress in 1972, has still not been ratified by the required two-thirds of the states, and while the gender wage gap is narrowing, women still earn approximately $0.81 for every $1.00 that men earn (http://www.dol.gov/equalpay/).

Critical Democratic Literacy and Civic Engagement

Civic engagement is a necessity for Critical Democratic Literacy (CDL). Democracy is the core of CDL, and democratic communities and nations require the involvement of its citizens. After the US Constitution was written, Benjamin Franklin was supposedly asked, "Dr. Franklin, what have you given us?" He replied, "A republic, if you can keep it." A republic, the type of representative democracy we have in the United States, requires citizens' constant attention and vigilance to ensure that the institutions of government, as well as our elected and appointed leaders, are doing what is best for the nation (or city or state) as a whole, as well as what is best for individual members of these communities. While knowledge of political institutions, historical and current issues, and concern for others are all important, without taking action and becoming involved in civic life, the "citizen" does not exist. While we may be citizens in the *legal* sense (i.e., citizen of the United States), if we do not engage, we are not citizens in the *practicing* sense.

Rationale for the Unit

Because being involved in civic life is so important, this unit draws students into an understanding of how others in the past have made a difference in their communities and nations and how students can become involved. Underlying these ideas is the notion that civic engagement is also reliant on civic virtue and the need to fully investigate and understand issues related to civic life. Thus these lessons highlight the role of researching into and understanding the past and its connection to today in order to participate in shaping the future. While the content and grade level focus for this series of lessons is different from those in Chapter 3, which focused on civic virtue, we would address civic virtue before civic engagement in any grade level.

Chapter Guide

This chapter moves through planning an entire unit on civic engagement for third grade. Any of the activities presented could be adapted for other grade levels as outlined in Chapter 7. Table 4.1 provides an overview of the unit components and the basic areas addressed across the unit. Both theory and practice are combined in order to (1) incorporate the theoretical framework of CDL, (2) represent the construction and teaching of lessons focused on social studies and literacy standards, and (3) meet the needs of elementary learners. Table 4.1 begins with civic engagement as the concept to be taught and then moves to an initial assessment before more specific lessons are designed. The assessment component focuses on both students and materials in order to adjust instruction based on teaching the students how to prioritize and sequence information. The unit is recursive and slowly builds up several areas of content and skills in order to integrate them into the large concept of civic engagement. The unit begins with a simulation lesson on voting as a form of civic participation. As the unit progresses, students engage in historical thinking as part of the social studies focus. This includes learning how to read primary source materials related to the WRM and exploring chronology by creating timelines by choosing significant events from biographies of women who worked and advocated

TABLE 4.1 Process guide for planning a unit on civic engagement

Civic Engagement	
Social Studies	*Critical Literacy*
School and family	Disrupting the commonplace Focusing on sociopolitical issues Taking action and promoting social justice
⬇	
Initial Assessment	
Students	
What do they know about voting as a type of civic engagement? What do they know about the concept of civic engagement? What do they know about the history of the WRM?	What do students know about the ideas of cause and effect? What do students know about taking action and promoting social justice?

Materials

I Could Do That! Esther Morris Gets Women the Vote
Elizabeth Leads the Way: Elizabeth Cady Stanton and the Right to Vote
Elizabeth Cady Stanton: Women's Rights Pioneer
Elizabeth Cady Stanton
Susan B. Anthony: Fighter for Women's Rights
Susan B. Anthony
Susan B. Anthony (TIME for Kids Nonfiction Readers)
Heart on Fire: Susan B. Anthony Votes for President
Lucretia Mott: Friend of Justice
Lucretia Mott
Lucretia Mott: A Photo-Illustrated Biography
Alice Paul

Standards

Social Studies Standards (C3 Framework)	Literacy Speaking & Listening Standards (CCSS ELA)	Literacy Reading Informational Text (CCSS ELA)	Literacy Writing Standards (CCSS ELA)
Civic and Political Institutions: D2.Civ.2.3-5. Explain how a democracy relies on people's responsible participation, and draw implications for how individuals should participate. **Processes, Rules, and Laws:** D2.Civ.12.3-5. Explain how rules and laws change society and how people change rules and laws. D2.Civ.14.3-5. Illustrate historical	**Comprehension and Collaboration:** CCSS.ELA-Literacy.SL.3.1.d Explain their own ideas and understanding in light of the discussion. CCSS.ELA-Literacy.SL.3.1.a Come to discussions prepared, having read or studied required material; explicitly draw on that	**Key Ideas and Details:** CCSS.ELA-Literacy.RI.3.1 Ask and answer questions to demonstrate understanding of a text, referring explicitly to the text as the basis for the answers. CCSS.ELA-Literacy.RI.3.3 Describe the relationship between a series of historical events, scientific ideas or concepts, or steps in technical procedures in	**Text Types and Purposes:** CCSS.ELA-Literacy.W.3.2.b Develop the topic with facts, definitions, and details. **Research to Build and Present Knowledge:** CCSS.ELA-Literacy.W.3.7 Conduct short research projects that build knowledge about a topic. CSS.ELA-Literacy.W.3.8 Recall information from experiences or gather information from print and digital sources;

(Continued)

TABLE 4.1 Process guide for planning a unit on civic engagement (*Continued*)

Standards			
and contemporary means of changing society. **Change, Continuity, and Context** D2.His.1.3-5 Create and use a chronological sequence of related events to compare developments that happened at the same time. D2.His.3.3-5. Generate questions about individuals and groups who have shaped significant historical changes and continuities. **Historical Sources and Evidence** D2.His.10.3-5. Compare information provided by different historical sources about the past.	preparation and other information known about the topic to explore ideas under discussion.	a text, using language that pertains to time, sequence, and cause/effect. CCSS.ELA-Literacy.RI.3.2 Determine the main idea of a text; recount the key details and explain how they support the main idea. **Range of Reading and Level of Text Complexity:** CCSS.ELA-Literacy.RI.3.10 By the end of the year, read and comprehend informational texts, including history/social studies, science, and technical texts, at the high end of the grades 2-3 text complexity band independently and proficiently.	take brief notes on sources and sort evidence into provided categories. **Production and Distribution of Writing:** CCSS.ELA-Literacy.W.3.6 With guidance and support from adults, use technology to produce and publish writing (using keyboarding skills) as well as to interact and collaborate with others. **Range of Writing:** CCSS.ELA-Literacy.W.3.10 Write routinely over extended time frames (time for research, reflection, and revision) and shorter time frames (a single sitting or a day or two) for a range of discipline-specific tasks, purposes, and audiences.

Learning Objectives
Students will:

Social Studies	Critical Literacy
• Explain the importance of voting. • Identify voting as one type of civic engagement. • Hypothesize why women did not get the right to vote until 1920.	• Students will explain the cause and effect of disrupting the commonplace and taking action and promoting social justice (e.g., the march for women's voting rights).

How Should I Get Involved in Civic Life? **63**

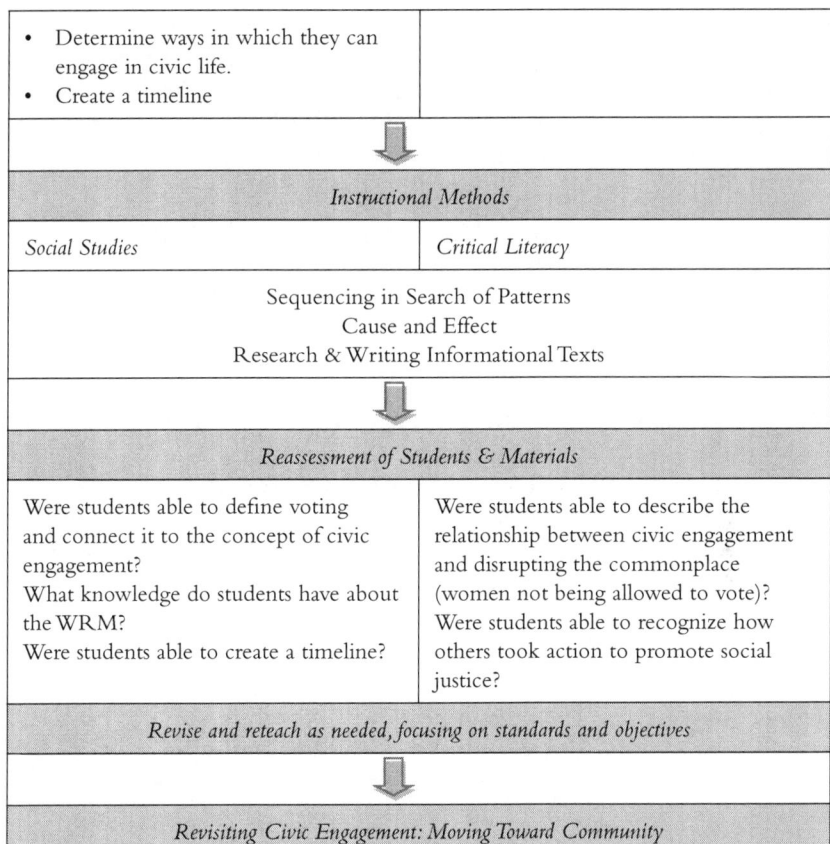

(i.e., types of civic engagement) expanding voting rights to women (i.e., suffrage). Finally, the students research a local and current issue in order to write a persuasive letter to an elected official, as a form of civic engagement.

Unit Narrative

This chapter introduces you to the third-grade classroom of Mr. Nuñez, a veteran teacher with bachelor's and master's degrees in elementary education. He teaches in a middle-class, ethnically diverse suburb in the far west and has 22 students. Teachers in Mr. Nuñez's school district are facing ever-increasing accountability demands, including high-stakes assessments in math and language arts. In particular, third grade is a testing year and his students are being assessed in language arts on reading and writing skills. Some of the emerging assessments are focusing third-grade reading and writing on analyzing complex text carefully and researching and writing subject-focused texts. Most third graders are fluent readers and writers; they can read and comprehend informational text and write short summaries of information. They usually need teacher support and modeling to produce complex oral and written responses to texts and other media. They, like most students, benefit from discussions of text, revision of ideas through the use of organizers, as well as evaluative tools to make decisions regarding new information. Many third-grade classrooms have a wide range of students with varying levels of reading and writing abilities. Mr. Nuñez has to carefully design lessons that accommodate his students so they can access all of the content while developing their literacy capabilities.

Civic Engagement: Preparing the Lesson

Reflecting on how the accountability movement has resulted in many of his colleagues abandoning social studies (Howard, 2003), Mr. Nuñez realizes that the best way he can continue to include social studies is to integrate it with literacy (Hinde, 2005). Mr. Nuñez values the citizenship education mission of social studies (NCSS, 2010) and, in particular, he wants his students to learn with an understanding that they have a civic responsibility to participate in their communities to make life better for themselves and others. His planning begins by placing the social studies concept of civic engagement at the center and noting that the most familiar form of civic engagement is voting, which is also something that his students have experienced in class. During their weekly class meetings, they had voted on a class mascot, field trip options, and which projects to share with families during back-to-school night. He thinks that this will be an easy connection and a good place to begin the lessons. He also realizes that it will then get more complicated as students are asked to apply their knowledge of voting to the more abstract concept of civic engagement.

As Mr. Nuñez considers his objectives, he focuses on two key ideas in social studies and reading and writing in literacy. First, in social studies, he wants his students to understand that voting is only one form of civic engagement and that there are other ways citizens exercise their responsibilities as members of a civic community. This is important for his students to understand because, as third graders, they may be able to vote and participate in decision-making in their classroom, but they cannot vote in public elections. His students could feel a few different ways about this, including that their thoughts and ideas do not count and that public issues that adults vote on do not affect children. Instead Mr. Nuñez wants his students to understand that they do have a voice and rights, and that they can make a difference, even if they cannot vote. One way of doing this is by having the students explore how different groups of people throughout US history who were not allowed to vote became engaged in civic life, persevered for decades, and eventually gained their right to vote. From Abigail Adams's letter in 1776 until the passage of the 19th amendment to the US Constitution in 1920, women fought for their rights for over 150 years. And that particular struggle happened long before any of his students were alive. Mr. Nuñez knows that it will be essential for his students to see themselves on the timeline of history.

Seeing themselves on the timeline of history can be directly related to sequencing textual events in literacy instruction. As a part of comprehension (Barton & Sawyer, 2004), sequencing is focused on understanding how events in a text occurred in particular order. By beginning with students' own lives, comprehension of the concept of sequencing builds on students' schematic understandings of time in relation to their own experiences. Sequencing is beneficial as an organizational frame and tool for students to learn so they can apply sequencing to texts they read and to their own written compositions. Researching and understanding how to interrogate specific topics is also a part of the third-grade standards and an integral part of learning about history while utilizing literacy skills.

This leads to Mr. Nuñez's second key idea in social studies—working with his students to develop a sense of chronology. He knows that the concepts of time, continuity, and change (NCSS, 2010) will be difficult for his young learners and must be scaffolded carefully. He has been working on this all year. For example, during the first week of the year, students made personal timelines as a way to introduce themselves to one another. In that lesson, students compared significant events and looked for cause and effect. For example, his student Holly listed "we moved to a new house when I was 7" as a significant event in her life. She also noted that "I had to change schools in second grade" as significant. As Mr. Nuñez helped her think about how these two important events in her life were related, Holly was able to determine that the move to a new house was a cause for attending the new school, the effect. This included the important aspect of putting these two events in chronological order so that the cause and effect could be better understood. Starting a new school did not cause her family to move; it was the other way around. This is an important part of historical thinking as students begin to look for patterns in history. Establishing historical patterns moves students beyond a listing of seemingly unrelated historical dates to understanding how historical events are related to one another. Seeing these relationships helps in building a historical narrative. As it relates to the students' personal timelines, each student used his or her own events to write an autobiography. The students used their own experiences but also interviewed family members, recorded notes, and searched for family artifacts to build their autobiographies. Writing research demands that students learn to move beyond personal narratives and begin to rely on facts and details. Using their timelines to construct autobiographies is the first step for third graders to begin understanding that each point they write about has to be based on a supported fact from their own experiences. By helping them see the relationships between the events, the autobiographies will become a researched, orderly depiction of their lives and not just a list of events. Holly's story will now not just list the two events of moving and starting at a new school, but she will be able to explain their relationship.

In a later unit on their school's history, students placed their personal timelines on a longer timeline that spanned the school's history. Through that experience, students learned that their school had been there before they were born; some of their parents also had attended the school when they were children; and that the part of the building where their classroom was located was added 10 years ago. Through all of these discoveries about their school, the students learned that the past went beyond their lives, but was still connected to their lives.

Timelines were also used throughout various readings to assist students in describing historical events to account for sequencing, pattern recognition, and cause and effect as they read both informational text and literature. Considering all of his goals, Mr. Nuñez decides to build on his students' experiences to introduce civic engagement and then bring in children's literature to look at women's rights across time. He will use the children's literature in addition to informational texts to also introduce chronology by building timelines.

Initial Assessment

In the following Friday's class meeting, Mr. Nuñez introduces the need for the class to decide on which song they will sing in the fall school concert from the three options provided by the music teacher. He tells the students that he is only going to allow students who are wearing orange, a fall color, to cast a vote. Only six of the students in class are wearing any orange and the remainder of the students immediately begin to protest that it is unfair that most of the class will be unable to vote. Mr. Nuñez has the students explain why they are upset and why his plan is unfair. Lauren and Noah explain that because they will all learn and sing the song, they should all get to vote. Other students nod their heads in agreement, and Mr. Nuñez asks if voting on the song is the students' right or responsibility. Most quickly agree that it is a right, but do not see it as a responsibility. Mr. Nuñez tells the students that he agrees that they should all have the right to vote on the song. Mr. Nuñez then asks the students if they get to vote on things outside of class. Some students mention that they sometimes get to vote in family meetings, while a few others mention voting at Scouts meetings or on athletic teams. Asking again if these instances of voting are rights or responsibilities, students again quickly point out that voting is a right. Aleeya offers that at a recent Scouts meeting, the troop had to vote on which nature project they would become involved in. In preparing to vote, they listened to guest speakers on the different projects, watched two films, and talked about how much time and money their troop would have to commit to each project. Aleeya tells her classmates that it was difficult and that it was important to "make a good choice." Aleeya added that knowing they could not do everything made her "think harder" and "be more serious" about how to vote. Mr. Nuñez picks up on this example, explaining that Aleeya provided a good example of voting as an important responsibility which could also be called a duty or obligation. Knowing that it is important for students to be able to stay on topic and communicate their own ideas orally, he continues the discussion in small groups building the students' speaking and listening skills in preparation for writing tasks later on in the unit. Small groups allow more students to engage in the discussion, and he is able to observe and listen to the students as he circulates around the room to each group. He then brings the class together to connect their ideas to their ongoing class examination of studying what it means to be a good citizen, noting that good citizens take their civic responsibilities, including voting, seriously. He also points out that throughout US history, many citizens could not vote, but that they found other ways to be good citizens.

Historical Thinking: Primary (Historical) Source Analysis

After the morning meeting, Mr. Nuñez continues his assessment, now focusing on students' understanding of chronology, as well as what they know about the WRM. He decides to have his students analyze an historical postcard about the WRM to assess their prior knowledge. Historical source work is a common part of an historian's methodology (VanSledright, 2004). In other words, one of the ways that an historian does his or her job is to analyze and interpret multiple primary sources, along with a wide variety of other sources, in order to build an interpretation of an event or era in history. Our intent is not to create expert or even mini-historians; rather, the intent is to introduce students to the unique type of critical thinking that is required when engaging in historical inquiry. When students analyze these sources they begin to understand that history (i.e., an interpretation of the past) is constructed and they begin to understand how historical accounts are created by historians. Students also have the opportunity to appreciate multiple perspectives, learning that multiple people perceive or experience an event or era differently. Understanding multiple viewpoints is also connected to critical literacy's goal of seeking out various points of view in order to make sound evaluations. This also addresses a misconception that primary sources are the best source of information about an event. Primary sources are typically defined as firsthand accounts of an event, like diaries, photographs, census records, etc. In reality, sometimes different people recall the same event differently, photographs are staged, and people are not truthful in letters; primary sources are not always the most reliable sources of information about the past. This is one of several misconceptions that Barton (2005) cautions us about as he offers ideas for thinking about what primary sources are and how they should be used in the classroom. In addition to the issue of reliability or accuracy, another caution is to believe that a source from the time period is always a primary source. In reality, it depends upon the historical question we are asking. If we want to know how West Coast newspapers reported on the White House protests by the suffragettes during the early twentieth century, those newspapers are primary sources. However, those same newspapers are secondary sources if our question is about the women's perspectives, especially if the story's author did not observe or interview women who were part of the protests. A related caution refers to collections of historical documents. For example, many of us have seen interesting collections of historical photographs and documents that have been woven together on a website or documentary. While the individual photographs or documents might be historical sources, someone, typically removed from the event, has made conscious decisions about which documents to include and exclude, how to organize them, and even what kind of music or narration accompanies them. When this happens, our primary sources have been interpreted into a particular narrative; they are no longer primary sources. As a result, Barton suggests we eliminate primary and secondary and just use the term *historical sources*. None of the above examples are reasons to avoid using historical sources in the classroom;

rather, they offer additional insights into wise practice. Working with and analyzing historical sources is one great way to build interest in an historical topic and engage students in inquiry. Mr. Nuñez is using historical source work in his initial assessment of his students' historical knowledge and understanding of chronology; it also builds student interest in the unit of study. Historians source or interrogate historical documents by asking and answering questions that focus on describing the content of the source and inferring or interpreting what the purpose of the source is, as well as what we should learn from the source. Mr. Nuñez displays a postcard from the early twentieth century titled "Votes for Women" (Figure 4.1) on the interactive whiteboard and asks the students some historical source analysis questions (Obenchain & Morris, 2015). The postcard has a picture of two children and a short poem about women's rights. This postcard was part of the WRM advocacy work in making sure that the issue of suffrage was kept in the public eye.

For the postcard, Mr. Nuñez asks the following questions:

1. What do the words on the postcard say? What are the people in the postcard doing? Describe their actions.
2. Do you think this postcard is from now or in the past? What in the postcard makes you think this?
3. What do you think the words at the top of the postcard mean?
4. What do you think the poem means? What in the poem makes you think this?
5. Why do you think this is an important postcard for us to look at?

Note that all of the questions require the students to reference the postcard. Further, the questions initially focus on a very literal description of the contents of the image. Typical of historical source work, a thorough examination of the historical document should be done prior to any interpretation. Focusing exclusively on a literal description is related to literacy comprehension when reading texts. Literal comprehension depends on a careful examination of the text as a primary source of information eschewing interpretation. After the questions requiring description, Question 2 moves into an interpretation, still using clues or evidence from the postcard. Through students' responses, Mr. Nuñez determines that the students have a sense of chronology as they can distinguish between past and present and are able to discern that the postcard is "from a long time ago" because it is "not in color" and "the boy's clothes are not what boys wear today." The students' answers directly reference the postcard. Questions 3 and 4 are also interpretive and rely on evidence in the document. It is also clear that the students were unaware that at one time women did not have the right to vote. Question 5 is an evaluative question, asking students to connect evidence from the postcard to a larger social context. Evaluation of the illustration and accompanying text mirrors inferential and critical comprehension goals where students are asked to move beyond the text to rely on additional sources of information and concepts to evaluate their reading. As students respond to this question, it is clear that

How Should I Get Involved in Civic Life? **69**

FIGURE 4.1 Primary source analysis

several students find it troubling that women could not vote at one time in history. They point out that it is unfair, just like what happened in the morning meeting, while others focus on their personal experiences with disagreements unrelated to the postcard's topic of voting. Some students disregard the text and remain mired in their interpretation of the illustration. Marin points out the last two lines in the poster, explaining that "if everyone has to follow the same laws, everyone should get to be part of making the laws." Eric asks, "Why couldn't women vote?" and Tara asks if women can vote now. These critical questions demonstrate the students' critical understanding of the unjust nature of denying women the right to vote. Focusing on sociopolitical issues at the institutional level also helps the students see beyond their own experiences so they can understand the powerful role laws have in society. The student discussion is also beneficial in requiring students to be prepared for participating in discussions, and for utilizing specific material as they explore topics in preparation for their research and writing activity later on in the unit.

As he reflects on his initial assessment of students' understandings of civic engagement and chronology, Mr. Nuñez determines that his students understand voting as a right, but are less familiar with voting as a civic responsibility and a form of civic engagement. In addition, students are able to articulate a general understanding of chronology by distinguishing between past and present, but have little prior knowledge of the WRM and at times they rely on personal opinions and guessing rather than the materials provided on the topic.

Standards

Mr. Nuñez's unit on civic engagement focuses on six standards from the Disciplinary Concepts and Tools section of the C3 Framework (NCSS, 2013). Specifically, he focuses on three civics standards that address the rights and responsibilities of citizens, as well as three history standards focused on the concepts of chronology and the skills related to primary source analysis. This fits with his intent to help the students see themselves as engaged and informed citizens. The companion Common Core State Standards for English/Language Arts (CCSS ELA) bring in the literacy standards related to sequencing and cause and effect to further assist students in connecting events to each other and understanding the relationships between events and larger historical issues with the overarching concept of civic engagement.

CRITICAL DEMOCRATIC LITERACY

Basing the lesson on civic engagement encourages CDL by ensuring that the skills the students are learning are contextualized in civic issues, rather than disconnected from their civic lives. This enables them to see the necessity of being both informed and engaged as members of a community.

TABLE 4.2 Learning objectives

Students will:	
Social Studies	Critical Literacy
• Explain the importance of voting. • Identify voting as one type of civic engagement. • Hypothesize why women did not get the right to vote until 1920. • Determine ways in which they can engage in civic life. • Create a timeline.	• Explain the cause and effect of disrupting the commonplace and taking action and promoting social justice (e.g., the march for women's voting rights).

Learning Objectives: When and How Should I Get Involved in Civic Life?

Mr. Nuñez decides to build the next integrated social studies and literacy lesson on the responsibility of civic engagement by exploring the history of the WRM. He is careful to connect the students' previous discussions to this addition to the lesson to build their understanding slowly over time. See Table 4.2 for a reminder of the unit's learning objectives.

Instructional Methods: Sequencing in Search of Patterns

How do people get their rights when they cannot access government through voting? Mr. Nuñez thinks about his students who are able to vote in the classroom, but not in the larger society. He wants them to understand the concept of civic engagement and that they have a civic responsibility to be engaged, even if they cannot vote. Working from the definition of civic engagement as the individual or collective actions that people take to make their communities better, he wants to design learning experiences that have students examine the concept in their own lives as well as throughout history. Knowing the importance of students' being able to determine not only the main ideas of texts but to rely on texts for information, he decides that a variety of children's biographies of women involved in the WRM will provide historical examples, using informational text, of what citizens can do even when they are denied their rights. In addition, Mr. Nuñez chooses biographies written in a chronological order, which he can use for developing timelines and furthering an understanding of chronology.

Building an Understanding of the Past Through Historical Thinking: Historical Significance and Chronology

Gathering his students on the reading carpet, Mr. Nuñez prompts his students to talk about some key ideas they remember about the timelines they made during the first week of the year. He begins by asking what the first thing was on their personal timelines. Ramon offers "my birthday" and Liz says "the day I was born." Taking a quick poll through a show of hands, all of the students agree that their birth was the first event on their timelines. Next, he asks, "What do you remember as some of the important events that you placed on your timeline?" Answers included, "I learned to ride my bike without training wheels," and "I went on an airplane for the first time." Mr. Nuñez connects their comments to historical significance (Seixas, 1997, 2004), reminding them that they did not put everything on their timelines, just the events that they believed were important. In addition, he points out that, besides the fact that all of the students agreed that their birthdate was a significant event, other significant events in their personal histories were different—not everyone included the birth of a sibling or starting school—and that different people believe different things are important. These are small points to students, but they help Mr. Nuñez continue to lay a foundation for historical thinking. As his students continue to study history, they will learn that different people and different groups, possessing different experiences and perspectives, find different events historically significant. This is part of realizing that historical narratives are constructed interpretations and that it is important to know about the author of the narratives. Comfortable with the students' understandings of timelines and chronology, Mr. Nuñez feels that the students are ready to move beyond their personal experiences and reference points and onto an in-depth study of historical content.

After the review of the students' personal timelines and their autobiographies, Mr. Nuñez asks about what they recall about the school's timeline they created. The students offered, "You [Mr. Nuñez] started teaching here before we even went to kindergarten," "the governor made a speech at the school when it first opened," and "when our city was smaller, our school had both elementary and middle school kids in it." Mr. Nuñez asks the students if they were present for any of those events in the school's history. Several students giggle at the question, reminding Mr. Nuñez that many of the events happened before they were born. This provides another opportunity for Mr. Nuñez to remind the students that they used and interpreted many historical sources of evidence (i.e., primary sources) like newspapers, yearbooks, and photographs to help them build an understanding of the history of the school.

With this, Mr. Nuñez introduces a book titled *I Could Do That! Esther Morris Gets Women the Vote* (White, 2005). He tells them that it is a biography and it is about a woman who lived a long time ago. He reminds the students that biographies are similar to their own autobiographies since they focus on the life of a person and they are based on extensive research. He also has a Web-based timeline-generating application open on the interactive whiteboard and has already entered Esther's birthdate of August 8, 1814 on the left side of the timeline. This is a direct connection to the students' timelines and their agreement that their birthdates were a significant event. He asks the students to listen for important events in Morris's life and to raise their hands when they hear one that they believe should be added. As he reads the book, students add several events, including "her mother died," "opened her own business," "got married to John Morris," "moved to Wyoming," "Wyoming women got to vote," and "Esther voted for the first time." Mr. Nuñez is using a timeline as a graphic organizer to help his students understand not just historical significance, but also to assist them in developing a sense of chronology. By determining which events are the most significant and then placing them in chronological order, students can begin to look for important patterns across time. These patterns may include patterns of cause and effect or patterns of continuity and change (http://historicalthinking.ca/historical-thinking-concepts). The students have experience with timelines, having done personal timelines and the school timeline. Mr. Nuñez knows that these earlier experiences were essential in building historical thinking skills using very familiar content. The familiar content helped students grapple with many of the abstract ideas of historical thinking, like historical significance and cause and effect. Building this new timeline of Esther Morris's life is the first time the students have built a timeline on someone and something so far removed from their own experiences. Mr. Nuñez also takes the opportunity to specifically point out that most of Morris's efforts toward getting women the right to vote happened before she had the right to vote. This reinforces two key points related to the civic engagement focus of the lessons. First, the timeline shows the order in which events happened so it is clearly visible that her efforts occurred prior to voting; and second, individuals can civically engage without having all of their legal rights.

Exploring the Women's Rights Movement Through Biographies

Having discussed the students' individual timelines and the school timeline, which extends beyond the life of one individual, and having made a timeline from the significant events in Esther Morris's life, Mr. Nuñez turns to having the students work in five small groups to examine the lives of several women involved in the early WRM (e.g., Susan B. Anthony, Elizabeth Cady Stanton, Alice Paul, Lucretia Mott). The heterogeneous grouping considers the varying reading levels typical of a third-grade classroom. By grouping students together with a variety of reading abilities, they can assist each other in accessing the content. Each group is given two to three children's biographies of varying levels of difficulty for the woman they are studying. Within each group, each student reads with a partner to answer two literal comprehension questions on a sheet of paper (Table 4.3).

TABLE 4.3 Biography timeline questions

1. Who was the main character in the book?
2. What are three things that happened in the book?
3. When did these three things happen?

Each group comes back together and each pair shares their answers to the two questions with the other students in their small group. After they have shared, the group creates a timeline of no more than four significant events. Choosing a limited number of events is purposeful as it requires the students to discuss the content of the texts, making conscious decisions about what is important or historically significant. Mr. Nuñez walks around the room, asking questions, and verifying that their timelines include events from the texts and images and are in chronological order. Mr. Nuñez is careful to remind students to verify their answers by going back to the texts they read. He also asks the students to create a visual element to accompany each significant event. Mr. Nuñez then pulls the class together, reminding the students about Morris's biography and all of the things she did to help get women the right to vote. He asks the students, back in their small groups, to evaluate which events that they have placed on their timelines relate to each woman working to get women the right to vote. Some of the groups need to make some changes on their timelines, having only chosen personal events as significant. This redirection and extra time reinforces the attention to the historical content under study, the WRM, and provides students with an opportunity to evaluate text using specific criteria.

Concept Web

A few days later, Mr. Nuñez draws a web on the board (Figure 4.2) and asks the students what it means to be on task in the classroom. Students offer a variety of ideas including "working hard" and "trying your best," among others. He then adds "participate in."

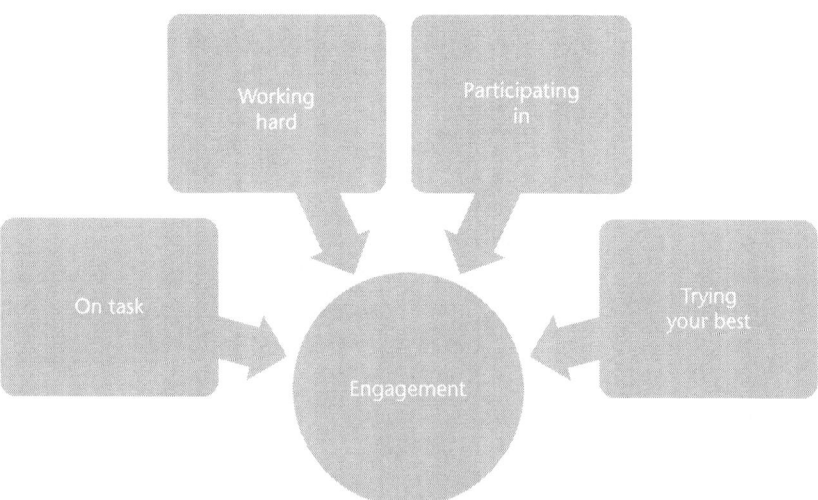

FIGURE 4.2 What does it mean to be "on task"?

How Should I Get Involved in Civic Life? **75**

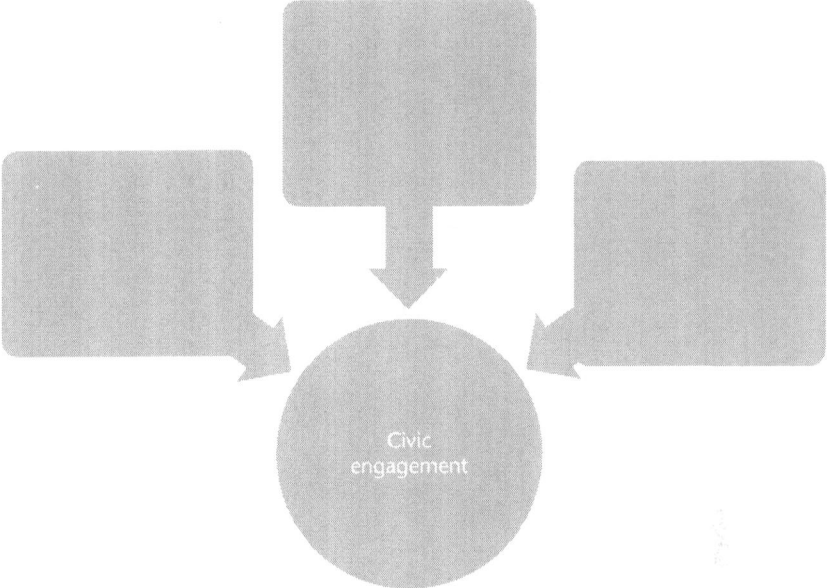

FIGURE 4.3 Civic engagement blank concept web

He then tells the students that being on task in the classroom, working hard on math, participating in class discussions, and trying your best in soccer is also called *engagement*, which he adds to the middle circle. As students prepare to line up for lunch, each one shares a statement beginning with "I am engaged in _____." This assists the students in understanding the term engagement and gives Mr. Nuñez an opportunity to briefly assess their initial comprehension of the concept of engagement. After lunch, Mr. Nuñez draws another web on the board (Figure 4.3) and places civic engagement in the center circle.

He explains that civic engagement is when people do things to make their communities better. He reminds the students about all of the women they have recently been learning about (e.g., Esther Morris, Susan B. Anthony). Mr. Nuñez asks the students to go back to their small groups and examine and discuss their timelines; they help decide which events to highlight, reminding each other that they have to circle events that show each woman helping other people. Mr. Nuñez pulls accurate examples from each group's timeline and adds it to the new web stating, "I saw one group circle an event where Elizabeth Cady Stanton gave speeches. That is a great example of how she did something to help women get the right to vote. What did Susan B. Anthony do to help others?" He continues to guide the students as they complete the chart together (Figure 4.4). Using a chart as a graphic organizer is key to helping students understand how to break complex ideas into manageable parts. They can use graphic organizers to

76 Teaching Critical Democratic Literacy

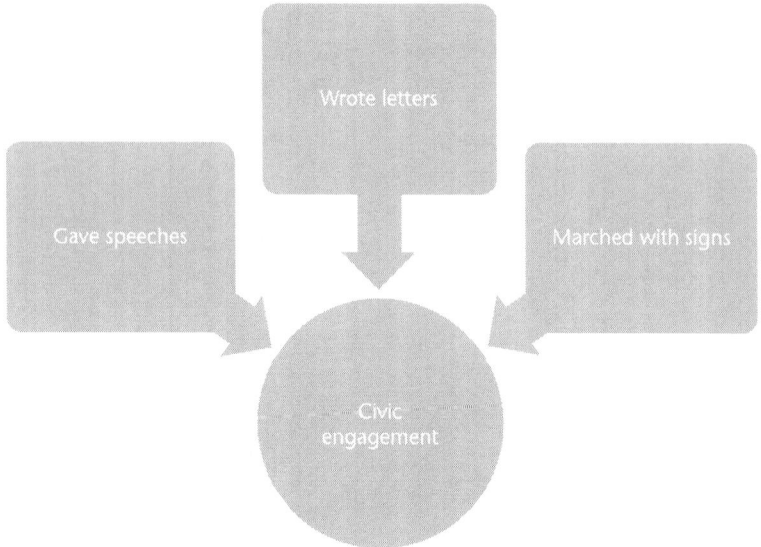

FIGURE 4.4 Civic engagement concept web

deconstruct texts and ideas as well as to formulate their writing as a prewriting activity.

Now that the students understand civic engagement in relation to the women suffragettes and specifically their civic engagement in women getting the right to vote, he returns to the idea of civic engagement within communities over time. Because third graders can struggle with the concept of time, he knows he has to scaffold based on their previous timelines about themselves, the school, and now the suffragettes.

Mr. Nuñez displays a large laminated timeline (Figure 4.5) that he created on the back wall of the classroom.

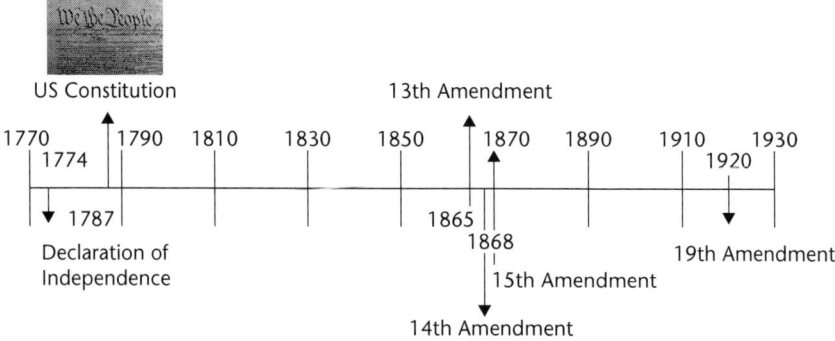

FIGURE 4.5 Claiming the right to vote timeline

The timeline begins in 1776 with the Declaration of Independence and ends in 1920 with the passage of the 19th Amendment to the Constitution which gave women the right to vote. It is evenly divided with one foot equaling 20 years, resulting in a nine-foot-wide timeline. This equal spacing on the timeline is important as students can easily see that while there were some periods in time when a lot of things happened close together, there were other periods of time in which nothing significant (in the topic under study) happened. While it might be easier and more visually pleasing to space the events themselves out, it is misleading and leads to a misunderstanding of the historical thinking concept of continuity and change. Mr. Nuñez has already entered significant events in US history related to individual rights, including ratification of the US Constitution, the Emancipation Proclamation, and passage of the 13th, 14th, and 15th Amendments. In addition to the title of these events, Mr. Nuñez adds a representative visual (e.g., a picture of the US Constitution). Working with one group at a time, Mr. Nuñez assists each group in placing the significant events in the life of the woman they studied on the timeline. Each woman is also assigned a different colored marker (e.g., Susan B. Anthony is red, Elizabeth Cady Stanton is blue) for adding the dates and writing the event. Groups also add the representative visual images that they created.

Once all of the individuals have been added, Mr. Nuñez asks the students to look at the timeline as a whole. He draws their attention to the different colored lines on the timeline and asks the students if the women were alive at the same time. They discover that Elizabeth Cady Stanton died before Alice Paul was born. While both of these women worked for the same cause of women's suffrage, they never worked together. This helps students understand the idea of collective action and how they may have worked together on the voting issue. Then he asks them if they noticed anything that was the same across the women's participation such as their engagement in meetings, letter writing, or marches. This further emphasizes the collective nature of their work together for the civic issue of voting. In addition, it creates the opportunity for students to understand that it took many years for women to obtain the legal and constitutional right to vote. They also discover that Susan B. Anthony and Elizabeth Cady Stanton died before women got the right to vote, reinforcing the idea that, as individuals, we do not always see the results of our work and that the causes we engage in may be complex and multifaceted. In addition, Mr. Nuñez has the students compare the significant events of the women's lives and the students quickly realize that the women, while all engaged in the WRM, did different things for the movement, and had very different lives. Recognizing that individuals and groups of individuals have different experiences and histories, just as their timelines vary, is essential. This creates the opportunity for students to practice exploring and understanding multiple perspectives, key to effective civic engagement. Also, it assists the students in learning how to gather information and relates it to the ideas of time, sequence, and cause and effect, key CCSS ELA standards for third graders.

> **CRITICAL DEMOCRATIC LITERACY**
>
> CDL requires an understanding of the concept of chronology in relation to prolonged civic engagement. Students can then learn to see how civic engagement, as well as civic virtue, is focused on the common good; or what democratic communities should be; and while individuals working on behalf of just causes may not directly or immediately benefit from their engagement, they can make a difference.

Once the students have worked through their timelines, Mr. Nuñez begins the writer's workshop process so they can construct their research reports. Knowing that his students will be assessed on their ability to write informative and explanatory texts, he works with the students over time using a writer's workshop model reinforcing drafting, revision, and editing. The framework for the students' writing begins with their biography timelines and moves to the civic issue of how women worked for their right to vote. Mr. Nuñez focuses on having students rely on facts, details, and the overall structural frame of writing researched informational text. He refers them back to their own timelines and autobiographies as models for their work. Students then are required to select an audience for their work and publish it within and outside of the classroom. They can choose to take their work home to share with their family, or they can share with another class at the school. This reinforces the purpose of writing for an audience and maintains the civic nature of being informed and sharing information.

"Reassessment" of Students and Materials

As Mr. Nuñez observes the students over the course of their writing and conferences with them individually, he discovers that while most of the students grasped the concept of civic engagement and were able to make connections across their timelines, others were only seeing the biographies as an isolated task and were only able to summarize the individual biographies of the people they read and wrote about. Their understanding of civic engagement was clearly related to voting and they did not understand how civic engagement could be relevant today. For example, his lessons did not connect to any current events. Therefore, the students were unable to identify how they might be civically engaged. Consequently, Mr. Nuñez decided to add to the unit in a way that would make the connections between the previous lessons and student experiences more concrete.

Revisiting Civic Engagement: Moving Toward Community

After the students shared their writing with their selected audiences, Mr. Nuñez brought the class back together to debrief. The students reported positively and they were clearly satisfied with being able to teach others about the topic of women voting. Ready to connect civic engagement to a current issue, Mr. Nuñez asked the students if they had heard about their city's plan to close a local skate park. The park is city-owned and used by city residents, so it is a public or civic issue. Some students were aware of the story and they shared their knowledge. Mr. Nuñez asked the students if they thought there was a way they might be able to participate in the discussion/debate/issue. Several hands were raised and students submitted ideas as Mr. Nuñez recorded them on the interactive whiteboard. He created a T-chart with two columns and listed pros and cons as students posed ideas. As a class, they used the interactive whiteboard, accessing local news sources in order to find more information about the skate park issue and how they could become involved. Just as critical literacy requires focusing on sociopolitical issues and taking action, the students are understanding how they can become engaged in their own communities.

One student suggests a protest at the park, just like some women in the WRM picketed in front of the White House. Mr. Nuñez notes that this is one option and that he is glad that the student remembered that historical event, but it might be too hard to do because the skate park is on the other side of town. He asks if the students remember anything else the suffragettes did in their work that the students might use. One student suggested writing a letter to someone in charge. Mr. Nuñez builds on this idea and suggests that the student write an opinion piece for the local newspaper supporting a point of view with facts, details, and supported reasons for keeping the skate park. Mr. Nuñez explained how the skate park was a city level decision and city decisions were made by the city council members. Over the course of the next week, Mr. Nuñez worked with the students to write a letter, and he connected the process to how engagement in the community is a necessary component of being a citizen.

Suggested Resources

Historical Thinking

The Historical Thinking Project (http://historicalthinking.ca/)

Timeline

Timeline and Map (http://www.britannica.com/EBchecked/media/51044/The-phrase-partial-suffrage-indicates-a-variety-of-limitations-imposed)

Women's Rights Movement

Department of Labor (http://www.dol.gov/equalpay/)
National Committee on Pay Equity (http://pay-equity.org/index.html)
The National Park Service's Seneca Falls, NY website (http://www.nps.gov/wori/historyculture/seneca-falls-in-1848.htm)
The National Women's History Project website (http://www.nwhp.org/resourcecenter/linkswomensrights.php)

The National Park Service's Women's History website and text of the *Declaration of Sentiments* (http://www.nps.gov/wori/historyculture/declaration-of-sentiments.htm)
Teacher Vision (https://www.teachervision.com/womens-history/video/73248.html#prettyPhoto)

Children's Biographies

Davis, L. (1998). *Lucretia Mott: A photo-illustrated biography*. North Mankato, MN: Capstone Press.
Hopkinson, D. (2005). *Susan B. Anthony: Fighter for women's rights*. New York, NY: Aladdin Paperbacks.
Malaspina, A. (2012). *Heart on fire: Susan B. Anthony votes for president*. Park Ridge, IL: Albert Whitman & Co.
Miller, C. C. (2006). *Elizabeth Cady Stanton: Women's rights pioneer*. Mankato, MN: Graphic Library.
Raum, E. (2004). *Alice Paul*. Portsmouth, NH: Heinemann.
Rice, D. H. (2011). *Susan B. Anthony* (*TIME for Kids* Nonfiction Readers). Huntington Beach, CA: Teacher Created Materials.
Sawyer, K. K. (1970). *Lucretia Mott: Friend of justice*. Lowell, MA: Discovery Enterprises.
Schlank, C. H. (1991). *Elizabeth Cady Stanton*. Lewisville, NC: Gryphon House.
Sterling, D. (1999). *Lucretia Mott*. New York, NY: Feminist Press.
Stone, T. L. (2008). *Elizabeth leads the way: Elizabeth Cady Stanton and the right to vote*. New York, NY: Henry Holt & Co.
Wallner, A. (2012). *Susan B. Anthony*. New York, NY: Holiday House.
White, L. A. (2005). *I could do that! Esther Morris gets women the vote*. New York, NY: Farrar, Strauss, & Giroux.

References

Barton, K. C. (2005). Primary sources in history: Breaking through the myths. *Phi Delta Kappan, 86*(10), 745–753.
Hinde, E. T. (2005). Revisiting curriculum integration: A fresh look at an old idea. *The Social Studies, 96*(3), 105–111.
Howard, R. (2003). The shrinking of social studies. *Social Education, 67*, 285–288.
National Council for the Social Studies. (2010). *National curriculum standards for social studies: A framework for teaching, learning, and assessment*. Silver Spring, MD: Author.
Obenchain, K. M. & Morris, R. V. (2015). *50 social studies strategies for K–8 classrooms*. Upper Saddle River, NJ: Pearson.
Seixas, P. (1997). Mapping the terrain of historical significance. *Social Education, 61*(1), 22–27.
Seixas, P. (Ed.), (2004). *Theorizing historical consciousness*. Toronto, Canada: University of Toronto Press.
VanSledright, B. A. (2004). What does it mean to think historically . . . and how do you teach it? *Social Education, 68*(3), 230–233.

5
HOW SHOULD I TALK ABOUT IMPORTANT CIVIC ISSUES?

A Fourth-Grade Unit on Civil Discourse

> *I would be glad even to know when any individual member thinks I have gone wrong in any instance . . . it would assist to guide my conduct . . . and to keep me to my duty . . .*
>
> *I will now add what I do not like.*
>
> Thomas Jefferson

Background Content for Teachers
Civic Concept: Civil Discourse

Civil discourse may be one of the earliest examples of what good citizens in a democratic state do. Civil discourse can be defined as learning through discussing (Kranich, 2010; Lindeman, 1935). It requires citizens who are well-informed and rational participants in thoughtful and meaningful conversations with one another to more deeply understand public or civic issues. A familiar example might be the New England town meeting in which all members of the community met to discuss issues and concerns relevant to the town or political community. In its most narrow sense and according to philosopher John Locke, what makes civil discourse different from other forms of discussion is the focus on public or civic issues (Walmsley, 1995). From this perspective, participating in a book club about a popular novel or discussing a new action movie is not *civil* discourse because these are not topics related to public or civic issues. However, for our purposes and for our elementary students, we utilize a broader perspective for understanding civil discourse. In order to move toward understanding, citizens must engage in discussions with those who believe both similarly and differently from one another. In particular, discussing important issues with people who think and believe differently allows us to better understand multiple perspectives, an important part of the social studies curriculum and of democratic citizenship education.

Engaging in civil discourse can be done orally and face-to-face, in writing, through visual representation like political cartoons and public art, and online. Each of these types of discourse requires different skills that should be explicitly taught. However, the core idea of civil discourse—citizens with different perspectives about an issue coming together to discuss those issues thoughtfully and in a well-informed manner—remains the same. Engaging in civil discourse may serve various purposes, but two purposes work well in the classroom when discussions are used as an instructional strategy (Parker, 2001). One type of discussion is called a *seminar*. The goal of this type of discussion is to gain a deeper understanding of an issue or text. A second type of discussion is called a *deliberation*, and the purpose of this discussion is to collectively make a decision about an action to take. Both types of discussions require civility; for elementary students this includes teaching students about active listening skills, how to develop and articulate an informed position, building upon others' ideas, and strategies for disagreeing with an idea and not a person. The goal is to gain insight, not victory (Parker, 2001, p. 111). These approaches also acknowledge that without substantive work on the part of the teacher, not everyone will enter the discussion on equal footing (Mazurana & Bonds, 2000). For various reasons, some students will tend to dominate a discussion while others will not engage. Civil discourse requires the informed participation of all, and that takes a great deal of work.

Historical Content: Deliberation About Adding a Bill of Rights to the New US Constitution

The first 10 amendments to the US Constitution are called the Bill of Rights and they were not originally part of the US Constitution. The term *amendment* means a change or addition and these 10 amendments were the very first changes to the new Constitution. Deciding whether to add a bill of rights was controversial at the time. There were two thoughtful and informed perspectives about whether to add a bill of rights. These two perspectives are generally represented through the differing positions of the Federalists and Anti-Federalists, the two major political perspectives of the time. Federalists believed in a federal system of government, which also implies a strong central or national government. This position is reflected in the design of the US Constitution (without amendments). While the document is careful to separate the powers of the national government among three branches (i.e., legislative, executive, and judicial) so no branch becomes too powerful, there is still substantial power invested in the national government. Remember that the Constitution was written because the Articles of Confederation, the first form of government in the new United States, did not work well and many believed it was because the central government did not have enough power. In the Articles, the focus was on the independence of the 13 states. The new Constitution was a reaction to that and the Federalists believed that the only way to secure the individual and collective political and social freedoms and independence that they had fought so hard for in the Revolutionary War was to create a strong federal government. James Madison, John Jay, and Alexander Hamilton were some of the Founding Fathers who were also Federalists. The Anti-Federalists, as their name implies, did not want a strong federal government. They were fearful that if they created a strong central government, it could potentially become like the British government and the American people would lose all of the rights and freedoms that they had won during the Revolutionary War. They believed that the three branches of the federal government all had too much power over the people and the states. Patrick Henry, Thomas Jefferson, and George Mason were well-known Anti-Federalist Founding Fathers. Anti-Federalists believed that the only way to prevent the new government, as outlined in the Constitution, from becoming too powerful and potentially taking away individual freedoms was to add a new section to the Constitution that detailed specific protections for citizens. A bill of rights would focus on explaining the civil liberties (i.e., the individual rights) of those who resided in the new nation. A bill of rights would set boundaries for the power and reach of the national government. Federalists did not think that listing these protections was necessary, believing that the Constitution already limited the powers of the federal government and did not need a bill of rights. As you can see from these brief descriptions, both positions were thoughtful, rational, and informed, but very different.

While the new Constitution, written in secret in Philadelphia during the summer of 1787, did not originally have a bill of rights, there was discussion of including one during the writing. However, the new Constitution was approved by the delegates and sent out to the 13 states for ratification. During the ratification process, which took three years, the discussion over a bill of rights became more important and concern grew that if a bill of rights was not included, some states might not ratify the new Constitution. Individuals representing both the Federalist and Anti-Federalist positions had to engage in civil discourse to resolve the issue. James Madison and Thomas Jefferson, two Founding Fathers, deliberated over many ideas related to the necessity of a bill of rights. James Madison, often called the father and architect of the Constitution, was present for all of the discussions during the summer of 1787. He took very careful notes during the Constitutional Convention, noting what was being discussed by whom, the issues, and the votes. These "Notes on the Constitution" are widely available. Thomas Jefferson was the ambassador to France during the writing and ratification of the US Constitution so he could not participate in person. However, Madison and Jefferson had a great respect for one another and Madison kept Jefferson apprised of the discussions during both the convention and ratification process through a series of letters. Jefferson, an Anti-Federalist, became very concerned that the Constitution had been approved without a listing of individual rights. He was afraid that if individual rights were not clearly explained, the federal government would abuse their power. The Anti-Federalists were concerned about the power of a central government and believed that the Constitution did not provide protection for individual rights. On the other hand, Madison, an early Federalist, supported the Constitution as a means of preserving the newly won independence of the United States, providing the strong central authority and structure that the Articles of Confederation lacked, and believed that a bill of rights was unnecessary and might actually create a more difficult position. Madison believed that our natural rights were so extensive that it would be impossible to list all of them. And, by including some rights (those to be protected), and leaving others out, the government might act in ways that did not protect the unlisted rights. Madison eventually changed his position and supported the inclusion of a bill of rights, in part because of a fear that the new Constitution would not be ratified at all. The Bill of Rights was eventually agreed upon and added through civil discourse—through the letters between Madison and Jefferson, the publication of the Federalist Papers and the Anti-Federalist Papers, and innumerable face-to-face discussions among many citizens.

Critical Democratic Literacy and Civil Discourse

Civil discourse can be viewed as a tool for effectively engaging in civic life. Critical Democratic Literacy (CDL) includes the ability to initiate and participate in discussions, debates, and decisions related to individual and community civic issues. Realizing the need for citizens to be adept at recognizing their role in being knowledgeable about topics that affect their lives and communities, CDL emphasizes the importance of participation through civil discourse.

Rationale for the Unit

Bringing civil discourse into the previous concepts of civic virtue and civic engagement provides students with the opportunity to both see their right and their responsibility to participate in discussions of what Parker (2012) terms enduring public issues. These kinds of issues have three key characteristics: (1) They are issues of civic or societal importance, like pollution or hunger; (2) informed and rational citizens disagree on how to resolve these issues; and, (3) these issues are called enduring because they have existed for a long time and societies have not solved them (the issues continue to be a problem). Given the importance of these issues, passion and emotion are not eliminated from civil discourse. Rather, passion and emotion are incorporated thoughtfully, respectfully, and rationally. Civil discourse can be seen as a means of avoiding uncivil and uneducated pontification, lecturing, or discounting other perspectives. When citizens are uncivil in their discourse, whether that be through yelling, personal attacks, or other intimidating behaviors, other citizens may be fearful of engaging in discourse. Refusing to listen or refusing to try to understand another's position is also uncivil. In addition, when citizens add the component of being uninformed in their discourse, it is very difficult to arrive at a deeper understanding. While we should all become more informed through the process of civil discourse, uninformed opinions expressed in an uncivil manner make it harder to achieve a deeper understanding or arrive at an informed decision. In addition to knowledge, there are numerous skills and dispositions students must learn in order to engage in civil discourse. In terms of skills, one example is active listening. Students should learn how to actively listen in order to avoid one-way communication. In these instances, students may only be waiting for a turn to talk and not actually listening to what others are saying. One example of a disposition is the valuing of multiple perspectives. Students should learn to respect and understand the multiple perspectives represented in discussions. Both of these examples, combined with being well-informed upon entering the discussion, will increase the likelihood that students leave the discussion as even more informed citizens. The lessons in this unit build on students' understandings of civic virtue and civic engagement by relying on the strategies of inquiry and deliberation. Students are guided through a process of seeing how civil discourse requires delving deeply into a civic issue and researching it before engaging in discussion, as well as being open to new information during the discussion, all in order to arrive at a decision about how to contribute to the resolution of the civic issue.

Chapter Guide

The chapter moves through planning an entire unit on civil discourse for a fourth-grade classroom. Any of the activities presented could be adapted for other grade levels. See Chapter 7 for additional information. Table 5.1 begins with civil discourse as the social studies concept to be taught and then moves to an initial assessment of students' background knowledge before more specific lessons are designed. Civil discourse is introduced by having students view two video clips in order to understand the basic notion of civil discourse. Table 5.1 provides an overview of the lesson components and the basic areas addressed across the unit. Both theory and practice are combined in order to (1) incorporate the theoretical framework of CDL, (2) represent the construction and teaching of lessons focused on social studies and literacy standards, and (3) meet the needs of elementary students. Once students comprehend the differences between civil discourse and uncivil discourse, the lessons move to the historical content of the Bill of Rights. The Bill of

TABLE 5.1 Process guide for planning a unit on civil discourse

Civil Discourse	
Social Studies	Critical Literacy
State and region	Interrogating multiple viewpoints

⬇

Initial Assessment	
Students	
What do students know about the Bill of Rights? What do students know about discussing topics with others?	What do students know about point of view? What do students know about supporting their points with facts?
Materials	
Primary sources: The Bill of Rights Letters between Jefferson and Madison about whether or not to include a bill of rights	Books: *The Bill of Rights: Protecting our Freedom Then and Now* *The Three Questions* *A Picture Book of Dolley and James Madison* *A Picture Book of Thomas Jefferson* *History for Kids: The Illustrated Lives of Founding Fathers-George Washington, Thomas Jefferson, Benjamin Franklin, Alexander Hamilton, and James Madison* *We the People: The Story of Our Constitution*

⬇

Standards			
Social Studies Standards (C3 Framework)	Literacy Speaking & Listening Standards (CCSS ELA)	Literacy Reading Standards (CCSS ELA)	Literacy Writing Standards (CCSS ELA)
Civic and Political Institutions: D2.Civ.4.3-5. Explain how groups of people make rules to create responsibilities and protect freedoms.	**Comprehension and Collaboration:** CCSS.ELA-Literacy. SL.4.1 Engage effectively in a range of collaborative discussions (one-on-one, in groups, and teacher-led)	**Key Ideas and Details:** CCSS.ELA-Literacy.RI.4.1 Refer to details and examples in a text when explaining what the text says explicitly and	**Text Types and Purposes:** CCSS.ELA-Literacy.W.4.1 Write opinion pieces on topics or texts, supporting a point of view with reasons and information.

D2.Civ.6.3-5. Describe ways in which people benefit from and are challenged by working together, including through government, workplaces, voluntary organizations, and families. **Participation and Deliberation: Applying Civic Virtues and Democratic Principles:** D2.Civ.10.3-5. Use deliberative processes when making decisions or reaching judgments as a group. D2.Civ.10.3-5. Identify the beliefs, experiences, perspectives, and values that underlie their own and others' points of view about civic issues.	with diverse partners on *grade 4 topics and texts*, building on others' ideas and expressing their own clearly. CCSS.ELA-Literacy.SL.4.1.a Come to discussions prepared, having read or studied required material; explicitly draw on that preparation and other information known about the topic to explore ideas under discussion. CCSS.ELA-Literacy.SL.4.1.b Follow agreed-upon rules for discussions and carry out assigned roles. CCSS.ELA-Literacy.SL.4.1.c Pose and respond to specific questions to clarify or follow up on information, and make comments that contribute to the discussion and link to the remarks of others. CCSS.ELA-Literacy.SL.4.1.d Review the key ideas expressed and explain their own ideas and understanding in light of the discussion.	when drawing inferences from the text. CCSS.ELA-Literacy.RI.4.2 Determine the main idea of a text and explain how it is supported by key details; summarize the text. CCSS.ELA-Literacy.RI.4.3 Explain events, procedures, ideas, or concepts in a historical, scientific, or technical text, including what happened and why, based on specific information in the text. **Craft and Structure:** CCSS.ELA-Literacy.RI.4.4 Determine the meaning of general academic and domain-specific words or phrases in a text relevant to a *grade 4 topic or subject area*.	CCSS.ELA-Literacy.W.4.1.a Introduce a topic or text clearly, state an opinion, and create an organizational structure in which related ideas are grouped to support the writer's purpose. CCSS.ELA-Literacy.W.4.1.b Provide reasons that are supported by facts and details. CCSS.ELA-Literacy.W.4.1.d Provide a concluding statement or section related to the opinion presented. CCSS.ELA-Literacy.W.4.2 Write informative/explanatory texts to examine a topic and convey ideas and information clearly. CCSS.ELA-Literacy.W.4.2.b Develop the topic with facts, definitions, concrete details, quotations, or other information and examples related to the topic.

(Continued)

TABLE 5.1 Process guide for planning a unit on civil discourse (*Continued*)

Standards			
	CCSS.ELA-Literacy.SL.4.2 Paraphrase portions of a text read aloud or information presented in diverse media and formats, including visually, quantitatively, and orally. CCSS.ELA-Literacy.SL.4.3 Identify the reasons and evidence a speaker provides to support particular points. **Presentation of Knowledge and Ideas:** CCSS.ELA-Literacy.SL.4.4 Report on a topic or text, tell a story, or recount an experience in an organized manner, using appropriate facts and relevant, descriptive details to support main ideas or themes; speak clearly at an understandable pace. CCSS.ELA-Literacy.SL.4.5 Add audio recordings and visual displays to presentations when appropriate to enhance the development of main ideas or themes.	CCSS.ELA-Literacy.RI.4.5 Describe the overall structure (e.g., chronology, comparison, cause/effect, problem/solution) of events, ideas, concepts, or information in a text or part of a text. CCSS.ELA-Literacy.RI.4.6 Compare and contrast a firsthand and secondhand account of the same event or topic; describe the differences in focus and the information provided. **Integration of Knowledge and Ideas:** CCSS.ELA-Literacy.RI.4.7 Interpret information presented visually, orally, or quantitatively (e.g., in charts, graphs, diagrams, timelines, animations, or interactive elements on web pages) and explain how the information contributes to an understanding of the text in which it appears.	CCSS.ELA-Literacy.W.4.2.d Use precise language and domain-specific vocabulary to inform about or explain the topic. CCSS.ELA-Literacy.W.4.2.e Provide a concluding statement or section related to the information or explanation presented. **Research to Build and Present Knowledge:** CCSS.ELA-Literacy.W.4.7 Conduct short research projects that build knowledge through investigation of different aspects of a topic. CCSS.ELA-Literacy.W.4.8 Recall relevant information from experiences or gather relevant information from print and digital sources; take notes and categorize information, and provide a list of sources. CCSS.ELA-Literacy.W.4.9 Draw evidence from literary or informational texts to support analysis, reflection, and research.

| | | CCSS.ELA-Literacy.RI.4.8 Explain how an author uses reasons and evidence to support particular points in a text. CCSS.ELA-Literacy.RI.4.9 Integrate information from two texts on the same topic in order to write or speak about the subject knowledgeably. | CCSS.ELA-Literacy.W.4.9.b Apply *grade 4 reading standards* to informational texts (e.g., "Explain how an author uses reasons and evidence to support particular points in a text"). |

Learning Objectives
Students will:

Social Studies	Critical Literacy
• Define the concept of civil discourse. • Participate in civil discourse. • Examine the reasons for the Bill of Rights. • Utilize the process of deliberation.	• Explain the importance of interrogating multiple viewpoints. • Participate in deliberation in order to understand the importance of multiple viewpoints.

Instructional Methods

Social Studies	Critical Literacy
Think-Aloud Social Studies/Historical Readers' Theater Inquiry Literacy Deliberation	

Reassessment of Students & Materials

Were students able to define and participate in civil discourse using deliberation? Were students able to provide a rationale for the Bill of Rights?	Were students able to explain the importance of interrogating multiple viewpoints? Were students able to understand the importance of multiple viewpoints through participation in civil discourse?

(Continued)

TABLE 5.1 Process guide for planning a unit on civil discourse (*Continued*)

Revise and reteach as needed, focusing on standards and objectives
⬇
Revisiting Civil Discourse: Moving Toward Community

Rights serves several purposes in the unit. It introduces individual civil rights to the students and serves to provide them with historical examples of civil discourse as it was used to construct the first 10 amendments to the US Constitution. Inquiry and deliberation follow as instructional strategies to support civil discourse, as well as a lesson on how inquiry and deliberation can be integrated. The First Amendment is utilized as an example of individuals' right to participate in civil discourse. Finally, students' understanding and skills are assessed as they research a current issue and use deliberation to come to a resolution in the spirit of the Founding Fathers and their civil discourse and deliberation about the inclusion of a bill of rights.

Unit Narrative

Mrs. Ramsey's fourth-grade classroom in a small city in the South has 30 students. She integrates social studies and literacy throughout the school year and her students have already worked through the concepts of civic virtue and civic engagement in the first half of the school year. As a fourth-grade teacher, she has students who are fluent readers and writers, but she has not worked on listening and speaking. Fourth-grade literacy skills are tightly focused on reading levels and how to write in response to prompts. Mrs. Ramsey wants to develop her students' ability to listen and participate in discussions with a concerted focus on using research and an integration of various sources to present ideas to others.

Civil Discourse: Preparing the Lesson

Understanding that civil discourse requires substantial preparation and practice for students, Mrs. Ramsey elects to rely on videos of examples and non-examples of civil discourse for the students initially. She then thinks about various ways for her students to engage in civil discourse practices. By teaching the unit midway through her school year, she can rely on her students' abilities to bring in civic virtue and civic engagement as they seek to add discourse to their schema and she is able to build on her students' research skills. She has spent the first semester of school working on teaching her students to research, read, and write about topics using informational texts. She now realizes that she can add the additional emphasis of listening and speaking to have students participate in deliberations. Mrs. Ramsey also expects the unit lessons to last three weeks to a month depending on the students' grasp of the content and the skills she is addressing.

Initial Assessment

For her spring unit on civil discourse Mrs. Ramsey wants to establish a fundamental understanding of the differences between civil discourse and what she terms, *uncivil discourse*. Her goal before delving into the historical content is to ensure that the students can easily determine the differences between the two. In order to set up the unit, she shows students two brief video clips of separate city council meetings, easily found on the Internet, asking the students to watch for what is similar and different about what people are doing in the two clips. The video clips clearly distinguish between civil and uncivil discourse. While the topics under consideration in the videos vary, the verbal tone and nonverbal actions demonstrate the differences between engaging in thoughtful, informed discussion and irrational, uninformed chaos. One clip demonstrates how council members debate a topic using *Robert's Rules of Order* to provide structure and equitable access to participation in the discussion. In addition, the council members in this clip clearly use appropriate evidence to support their points. The second video clip shows city council members raising their voices, not actively listening as evidenced by speaking over one another, and leaving the room instead of listening to their colleagues. Mrs. Ramsey uses specific prompts to focus the students during the initial whole class discussion. She asks them to describe how the two videos were similar ("they were both about meetings") and how they were different ("people weren't nice in the second video"). She introduces and briefly defines the terms civil (polite, respectful) and uncivil (impolite, rude), asking the students to determine if people were acting civil or uncivil in each of the video clips.

Civility is one essential component in understanding the civic concept of civil discourse. As the students continue to discuss their observations, Mrs. Ramsey ties their points to their personal experiences by asking them if they have ever argued or disagreed with someone. Moving from a whole class discussion to partner talk, the students share examples of civil and uncivil discussions they have participated in. She listens to one pair discuss an argument they overheard on the school playground about taking turns on the swings and how two students were yelling at each other. The students decided it was civil because no one cried and no one got hit. Another pair talks about the same example, but they decided it was uncivil because there was a lot of yelling and no listening. Mrs. Ramsey then asks the students to also share examples of informed and uniformed discussion that they have participated in. Being an informed discussion participant is a second essential component of understanding what civil discourse is, as well as what is required of those who participate in civil discourse. Throughout the week, Mrs. Ramsey refers to the idea of civil discourse by bringing in read-aloud picture books and using the terms *civil, informed*, and the larger concept *civil discourse* as she handles conflicts between students during the school day. She maintains the same vocabulary as she asks students, "Was that a civil conversation about who should get to use the basketball court or was that

TABLE 5.2 Civil discourse T-Chart

Civil Discourse	Uncivil Discourse
Talking calmly	Yelling
Listening to others	Not listening to others
Looking at the talker	Not looking at the talker

an uncivil conversation?" She tracks her students' application of the term *civil* over the week and then moves onto the formal lesson. She brings in questions about how students have dealt with people they disagree with and refers back to the city council videos. The students assist her with composing a class definition of civil discourse and uncivil discourse. They create a T-Chart (Table 5.2) with a bulleted list of attributes defining both concepts, as they understand them at the beginning of the lesson. The students create a dichotomous relationship between the two ideas, and Mrs. Ramsey recognizes their need to classify the terms separately.

Standards

After this initial assessment, she looks to the standards as she adds in content. Mrs. Ramsey's unit on civil discourse focuses on four standards from the Disciplinary Concepts and Tools section of the C3 Framework (NCSS, 2013). Specifically, Mrs. Ramsey focuses on four civics standards that address the areas of *Civic and Political Institutions* and *Participation and Deliberation: Applying Civic Virtues and Democratic Principles*. These four standards address when, where, and how citizens should engage in civil discourse. Every fourth-grade Common Core State Standards English/Language Arts reading informational text and writing standard could apply to this unit; Mrs. Ramsey attends to the reading and writing standards that align well with reading for understanding and writing using resources. Listening and speaking apply as well, and she integrates them into the oral discourse opportunities embedded in the lessons.

Learning Objectives: "How Should I Talk About Important Civic Issues?"

Inquiry and deliberation are the cornerstones for the unit. Therefore, Mrs. Ramsey aligns the notion of civil discourse to the social studies objectives and instructional strategies of inquiry and deliberation. Fourth graders will use their research reading and writing skills to frame an issue of civic concern and to engage in a deliberation in order to demonstrate their ability to define and engage in civil discourse. Table 5.3 provides a reminder of Mrs. Ramsey's social studies and literacy objectives.

TABLE 5.3 Learning objectives

Students will:	
Social Studies	Critical Literacy
• Define the concept of civil discourse. • Participate in civil discourse. • Examine the reasons for the Bill of Rights. • Utilize the process of deliberation.	• Explain the importance of interrogating multiple viewpoints. • Participate in deliberation in order to understand the importance of multiple viewpoints.

Instructional Methods

Establishing students' command of civil discourse, Mrs. Ramsey adds historical content by reading the book, *The Bill of Rights: Protecting Our Freedom Then and Now* (Sobel, 2008). The book explains the relationship of the Bill of Rights to the US Constitution. Mrs. Ramsey hones in on the chapters titled "Many Disagreements," "The People's Rights, and "Adding the Bill of Rights" to demonstrate how the framers of the Constitution spent time discussing their ideas and differences with one another. In general, the book outlines the differences between the Federalist and Anti-Federalist positions about the inclusion and content of a bill of rights. It also shows how strongly people on each side of the issue believed in their particular position, as well as their ability to come to a decision that they all believed was best for the United States.

After reading the book, she leads a short discussion about James Madison and how he changed his mind about adding the Bill of Rights to the Constitution. Initially, Madison, a Federalist, believed that a bill of rights was unnecessary. One reason was that he believed that individual rights were so broad and encompassing that there was no way to list them all; and whatever they did not list might be seen as a right that citizens did not have. After much civil discourse with Thomas Jefferson and others, Madison drafted a bill of rights. In other words, after gaining new information through discussion and study, Madison changed his mind. This is an important point in teaching students about civil discourse, specifically, and discussions, more broadly. We enter the discussion with an informed perspective, but we also become more informed through the process of participating in the discussion.

To offer a written example of civil discourse, Mrs. Ramsey introduces copies of letters exchanged by James Madison and Thomas Jefferson. The letters illustrate the many perspectives of both Founding Fathers and while the text is difficult due to the vocabulary and grammatical structure, Mrs. Ramsey reads along with the students and uses a think-aloud instructional strategy to translate the main points of the letter excerpts related to the Bill of Rights. She brings in the connection between Madison's and Jefferson's letters and the concept of civil discourse by explaining that the two friends did not agree about the need for the United States to have a bill of rights as part of its new Constitution. As she finishes the reading, Mrs. Ramsey shares some biographical information about Madison and Jefferson. She shares two short biographical books and places them in the classroom library. Her Bill of Rights resource table is covered with books at various reading levels, videos, photos, and primary source documents related to the Bill of Rights with special attention to Madison and Jefferson. She encourages her students to explore these resources over the following days.

Social Studies/Historical Readers' Theater Lesson

After a few days, she brings the students together to review the relationship between Madison and Jefferson and to introduce a social studies/historical readers' theater (SS/HRT). Readers' theater is fairly common in the literacy curriculum, often used to enhance fluency and comprehension of texts that students are reading. Teachers take a text and adapt the text into a script. The key to readers' theater is that the script provides a means for students to reread the same text multiple times with the other characters. These repeated readings provide the students with the opportunity to discuss how a character might talk in relation to their tone of voice and nonverbal body language. The rereadings bring students' attention to how the characters are thinking and why they are interacting in specific ways. Readers' theater scripts are meant to be read to an audience, not to be memorized. The reliance on the script also incorporates specific vocabulary and grammatical patterns into the students' oral language knowledge. Teachers have to take care to carefully match students' reading levels with their character parts and adjust the script to meet the students' needs.

CRITICAL DEMOCRATIC LITERACY

Understanding how different citizens and groups have multiple, informed, and different perspectives is essential to CDL. This understanding is foundational in recognizing the need to talk with people who believe differently in order to make the best and informed decisions for the community.

Mrs. Ramsey is going beyond the traditional literacy purpose to instead incorporate SS/HRT, adding an explicit social studies dimension and purpose. In SS/HRT, fluency and comprehension are addressed, but when the scripts are chosen or written, they are done so with specific social studies content goals in mind. The structure of a SS/HRT is very similar to that of a literacy-only readers' theater. It includes either finding or creating a script from an existing text, such as historical sources of evidence (i.e., primary sources) like letters, a diary, or newspapers. Important documents like the Preamble to the US Constitution, the United Nations Convention on the Rights of the Child, and the Pledge of

Allegiance could also work. Historical fiction is also another appropriate source for creating an SS/HRT script. The text choice depends upon the literacy and social studies goals and learning objectives. One SS/HRT goal that crosses both literacy and social studies is for students to recognize and value diverse perspectives. For a history lesson, we could modify this broad goal to understanding historical perspectives, a key goal and concept within historical thinking (Seixas & Morton, 2012). In social studies, SS/HRT may also advance learning objectives related to specific social studies concepts like interdependence, justice, and movement, etc. The best SS/HRT scripts are teacher-created because they are directly matched to the academic standards and learning objectives that the lesson addresses. In addition, by creating your own, the social studies goals of the lesson are where the process begins. However, there are numerous existing readers' theater scripts available online and in print. In creating a SS/HRT script, there are several considerations to keep in mind beyond the importance of the learning objectives (Obenchain & Morris, 2015). Once the social studies goals, content, and any specific social studies concepts have been identified, choose a text (e.g., the Pledge of Allegiance) or text excerpts (e.g., just the Preamble to the Declaration of Independence) that provide important content or an illustration of a concept or even a skill under study. Examine and then divide the text so that there can be several readers. For some children's literature (e.g., historical fiction), there will already be some natural divisions because there are different voices. The children's book *Pink and Say* (Polacco, 1994) already has distinct roles because there are several characters in the book. However, some texts, like the Pledge of Allegiance, do not have natural divisions. In this case, divide the text into natural pauses (e.g., ends of sentences, paragraphs, and ideas). In this example, the specific roles could be Narrator 1, Narrator 2, Narrator 3, etc. Students are then assigned a role in the script and have ample time to practice their part by reading aloud. SS/HRT is not about memorization of a script, props, costumes, or about acting. It is about advancing the literacy and social studies academic goals and objectives of the lesson. However, it is appropriate that students consider inflection and tone as they practice, as this is an opportunity to deepen their understanding of the character they represent, the content of what they are reading, and the historical or socio-political context of the text. The practice also supports students in advancing their fluency and reading comprehension. In addition, the practice should include conversations and possibly background resources that connect the script to the larger social studies content and concepts under study. Once well-practiced, students, typically in small groups, perform their script in varied settings. Mrs. Ramsey follows a very similar process in the SS/HRT she creates for her students.

Mrs. Ramsey has constructed a SS/HRT script that she distributes to her students. She built the script from the letters between Jefferson and Madison that she identified as supporting her students' learning of the historical content of the Bill of Rights and the civic concept of civil discourse. Mrs. Ramsey created the script by placing the letters in chronological order, using specific excerpts and then writing the narrative transitions to assist the students with historical and chronological context. They all do a group shared reading as Mrs. Ramsey pauses to review points about the disagreement between the two Founding Fathers; this is where she introduces and reinforces the historical content and civic concept under study. She tells the students that Jefferson was in Paris during the time that Madison and other political leaders, back in the US, were discussing adding the Bill of Rights to the Constitution. So the letters, in the form of a SS/HRT script, show how they were able to engage in civil discourse in a written format. After the group reading, Mrs. Ramsey divides the students into groups of five, as her script has two Jefferson readers, two Madison readers, and one narrator. The student groups then sit around the room reading the script together and they decide on parts to play and begin to rehearse. Each script has a narrator who introduces the letters with dates and then a few brief statements that cover the points Madison and Jefferson discuss. Over the week, during free reading time, the small groups rehearse. They also select audiences for their performance. Some groups go to other classes to perform the short SS/HRT and others select specific individuals or groups such as the principal, the cafeteria workers, etc., as their audiences. Each student group consists of readers with various reading levels and students are encouraged to read chorally to assist each other. They end their presentations with a short explanation of civil discourse based on their class definition built from the T-Chart. They also ask members of their audience to offer their own examples of civil discourse and uncivil discourse. This provides an additional example for the students to reflect upon their understanding.

The following week, Mrs. Ramsey brings the T-Chart with the class definitions of civil discourse back to the students. She asks them to recall and share some of the examples they heard from their historical readers' theater audiences. Susanna shares that the first grade her group presented to explained that their weekly class meetings were civil discourse because they took turns talking. This provides an opportunity for Mrs. Ramsey to remind her students of the civil discourse between Madison and Jefferson and highlight how these examples illustrate a reliance on knowledge (i.e., being informed) in addition to their civility. Mrs. Ramsey knows that civil discourse is predicated on knowledge of the issue under deliberation. She tells the students the importance of adding in knowledge and understanding to their definition, and, with student assistance, they revise the T-Chart (Table 5.4).

The students connect the new aspects of the definitions of civil and uncivil discourse to topics they are familiar with such as how to best get to the playground and how to be safe riding your bike to school. Mrs. Ramsey allows the students to orally explain their ideas about the best route to the playground from their classroom. Cory and Gavyn advocate for the route through the cafeteria. Cory says, "I like to go through the lunch room." Mrs. Ramsey prods Cory to explain why he likes that route and he replies, "It is the best way." She nods and

TABLE 5.4 Revised civil discourse T-Chart

Civil Discourse	Uncivil Discourse
Talking calmly	Yelling
Listening to others	Not listening to others
Looking at the talker	Not looking at the talker
Relying on information	Relying on feelings
Trying to understand all sides	Trying to tell only your side
Trying to come to an agreement	Trying to win

asks him why it is the best way, and he says it is under the covered sidewalk. Alternatively, Jake and Ashley advocate for the route through the school garden. Ashley says, "It is better to go through the school garden because it is faster." Mrs. Ramsey acknowledges their ideas, asking questions that require them to use specific information. Soon the class is deliberating on their own, asking questions of one another. Mrs. Ramsey praises their discussion contributions and connects their work to civil discourse using the chart. She reminds them that they are knowledgeable about the school and their knowledge helps them make relevant contributions to the discussion. She reiterates the importance of civil discourse as not only being respectful but also being knowledgeable. What Mrs. Ramsey discovers from this specific discussion about getting to the playground is that students are relying on information they already possess. They are not gathering new information or even checking to see if their information is correct. This prompts Mrs. Ramsey to include an inquiry lesson.

Inquiry Literacy Lesson

Bringing the students to understand the role of inquiry in becoming a more informed decision-maker is key. Mrs. Ramsey uses the book *The Three Questions* (Muth, 2002) to introduce inquiry. The book follows Nikolai, a boy looking for guidance in doing the right things. The book ends by highlighting the importance of acting thoughtfully and for the good of others. In the book, others are called "for the one who is standing at your side." She connects the book to the broad idea of being a member of a community, as well as to the idea of inquiry—asking difficult questions that do not have a single or simple answer. While Nikolai asks three questions as he tries to figure out what he should do, the students should ask questions of themselves, of others, and of texts before they make a decision. Asking questions and gathering and evaluating information is how one becomes informed, and is the basis of inquiry and research. As previously covered, Madison and Jefferson engaged in a long and thoughtful deliberation based on gathering, sharing, and evaluating information. They did not make the decision to include a bill of rights, or which rights, for that matter, without thinking through their decisions and discussing their ideas. Mrs. Ramsey emphasizes the need to prepare before engaging in deliberation and sets up an activity that guides students through an inquiry process (Obenchain & Morris, 2015). She sets up the following steps by giving each student a folder with five separate sections labeled as follows:

1. Identify the issue.
2. Create a hypothesis.
3. Collect information.
4. Evaluate the information.
5. Test the hypothesis.

These sections represent a typical inquiry cycle common to the science curriculum. However, the inquiry process can be modified to encourage the development of critical literacy, an understanding of the tentativeness of knowledge (e.g., our individual understanding of an issue or event), and an appreciation for multiple perspectives. Inquiry literacy topics typically deal with social or historical issues in which multiple right answers are appropriate. This is consistent with how Mrs. Ramsey approaches inquiry literacy. The standards echo these ideas as they ask fourth graders to be able to recall relevant information, categorize the information, and then orally report and explain their research.

The students listen as Mrs. Ramsey describes how Madison and Jefferson identified the issue of how best to protect the individual rights of citizens in the new United States. She provides a graphic organizer to facilitate her explanation and organize the information for her students (Table 5.5). She noted that Madison hypothesized that the Constitution secured the rights without an additional bill of rights; meanwhile Jefferson hypothesized that a bill of rights was needed. They each collected information from each other, as well as others, evaluated the information, and tested their hypotheses. In the end, Madison revised his initial hypothesis, agreeing with Jefferson that the Constitution did need a bill of rights.

Mrs. Ramsey then turns to more current uses of inquiry literacy. She discusses her own inquiry into the current issue of whether or not the minimum wage should be raised. She shares the inquiry process she follows in order to be an informed participant in the civic issue of changing laws to pay workers more money. Mrs. Ramsey shares the contents of her "Minimum Wage" folder. It includes news stories about workers protesting outside of various businesses that pay the current minimum wage, an interview with a business owner who is concerned about the consequences to his business of raising the minimum wage, government statistics on how much money an individual and a family need in order pay all of their bills, and a page that has several URLs. Mrs. Ramsey explains that these links take her to other news stories, videos of congressional hearing testimonies, and debates between experts. Many of these resources reflect a person

TABLE 5.5 James Madison and the Bill of Rights inquiry

Is a bill of rights necessary in the new Constitution?		
Initial Hypothesis A bill of rights is not necessary in the US Constitution.		
Summary of information: People are entitled to a written protection of their rights.	Summary of information: If any rights are written down, a bad government might think these are the only rights to protect.	Summary of information: Some states are reluctant to ratify the new Constitution without a bill of rights.
Source of information: Thomas Jefferson letter	Source of information: Alexander Hamilton in Federalist No. 84	Source of information: Madison's experiences trying to get his home state of Virginia to ratify the Constitution
Does this evidence support or refute my hypothesis? Refute	Does this evidence support or refute my hypothesis? Support	Does this evidence support or refute my hypothesis? Refute
Revised Hypothesis		
A bill of rights is appropriate to protect individual rights and is necessary to ratify the Constitution.		

or group speaking out for their perspective on this civic issue. She shares with the students that she only chose to collect resources that represented people and groups engaging in civil discourse. Mrs. Ramsey also tells the students that the workers can decide to speak out on their own or they can engage with others to participate as a group, but either way, they have to be informed. They have to listen to other perspectives, including what might be a reasonable increase. Her modeling and working through a think-aloud of her own inquiry leads the students to think about topics they or their family members have researched.

Some students make simple connections about how they have researched which video game to purchase or which car their families decided to buy. Mrs. Ramsey acknowledges their connections and works to build up the idea that inquiry in relation to civil discourse should be on a topic that is a social issue for a group in society. She reiterates how minimum wage affects people who have no power to request more money. The powerful corporations that determine salaries can legally pay their workers a wage that does not provide them with enough money to take care of their families. The students start to connect the critical perspective of inquiry as it relates to how to empower people who have no means to change their situations.

Evaluation

Now that the students have moved from a basic understanding of what civil discourse is to recognizing their need to incorporate the inquiry literacy process so that they can be informed participants when they engage in discourse, Mrs. Ramsey prepares the students to deliberate about a current school issue—students bringing cell phones to school. She selects this topic because it is currently under discussion by the school district, and the students are aware of this. Further, the issue can be framed as balancing individual rights (e.g., my right to have my cell phone) and the common good (e.g., it disrupts learning). Balancing individual rights with the common good is an enduring issue in society and an idea that Mrs. Ramsey frequently brings into lessons. Mrs. Ramsey introduces the issue by sharing three pieces of information: (1) the school district's proposed policy on cell phones; (2) a news article that is against students bringing cell phones to school; and (3) a brief video of an expert stating the reasons students should be allowed to have cell phones. Students are then asked to write their own initial hypothesis to the question: Should cell phones be allowed in schools? Knowing that writing hypotheses is new to her students, she provides a simple template for them (Table 5.6).

Mrs. Ramsey's plan is to have the students separate into a pro/con side. However, based on their initial hypotheses, all of the students elect to support the use of cell phones in school. Instead of forcing the students to advocate a position they do not believe in, especially in their first inquiry literacy experience, Mrs. Ramsey decides to participate in the inquiry literacy process herself, supporting her hypothesis that students should not be allowed to have cell phones in school.

CRITICAL DEMOCRATIC LITERACY

Citizens must engage and discuss from an informed perspective built through a purposeful examination of multiple, reliable, and conflicting sources of information. Otherwise, they rely only on emotions, personal experiences, and sources that serve only to confirm what they already believe.

TABLE 5.6 Cell phone hypothesis template

Students ____should/should not____ be allowed to have cell phones in school.

Over the course of the next week, students fill their folders with research from websites, newspaper articles, and news videos. Over time they are interpreting information together and working on their understandings of the issue. They engage in discussions in small groups and the whole group, and they revisit their sources periodically to support their points. The reliance on sources as they discuss is a big step in their understanding the importance of not only relying on personal opinion. They read views about cell phones in schools that they do not agree with. They have to explain these views and understand them well enough to present them to their small groups. One group decides to interview the principal about her position on cell phones in school, and another group interviews the technology teacher about his thoughts on the educational use of cell phones in the classroom. With reminders from Mrs. Ramsey to think about finding the most reliable information, students meet in their table groups and begin to organize their data. The folders serve as an organizational tool initially, but partway through the process Mrs. Ramsey takes an opportunity to show the students her own folder. She shows them each source and how she is starting to summarize her sources so she can evaluate them. Similar to the Bill of Rights hypothesis graphic organizer, Mrs. Ramsey creates an expanded version for the students to use in their cell phone inquiry (Table 5.7).

TABLE 5.7 Cell phone hypothesis graphic organizer

Should students be allowed to have cell phones in school?		
Initial Hypothesis Students <u>should not</u> be allowed to have cell phones in school.		
⬇		
Summary of information:	Summary of information:	Summary of information:
Source of information:	Source of information:	Source of information:
Reliability of information:	Reliability of information:	Reliability of information:
Most important points:	Most important points:	Most important points:
Does this evidence support or refute my hypothesis?	Does this evidence support or refute my hypothesis?	Does this evidence support or refute my hypothesis?
⬇		
Revised Hypothesis		

She adds a new section about the reliability of the source, as well as an evaluative section where she records notes that help her decide which sources have the best information to help her formulate her position. She shares with her students that as she has gathered and evaluated information, her hypothesis has become more specific; she now has evidence for why students should not bring cell phones to school. The students return to evaluating their sources, formulating their positions, and refining their hypotheses. Mrs. Ramsey uses this activity to assess students' oral language, ability to extract facts from texts and other sources, and their ability to evaluate sources and write an argument.

Reassessment of Students and Materials

After the student groups have completed their research, each student writes two paragraphs stating their initial hypothesis, summarizing their best evidence both in favor of and against their hypothesis, and then stating a new, more informed, and refined hypothesis. Each student has the opportunity to orally present his or her paragraph to a small group of students and answer questions from their peers. This provides students with an early experience of presenting and defending their position. Students then turn in their individual folders, and Mrs. Ramsey matches student written work with her anecdotal notes in order to assess each student's understandings.

Revisiting Civil Discourse: Moving Toward Community Through Deliberation

Once the students have demonstrated their ability to use inquiry to research an issue, it is crucial that they learn how to apply their knowledge and engage in civil discourse. Mrs. Ramsey uses a deliberation strategy, which has the goal of coming to a collective decision through discussion (Parker, 2001). Mrs. Ramsey realizes that she has to make a major modification to the strategy. Typically, there are at least two positions in the discussion with a relatively equal number of advocates for each position. However, all of her students want the right to bring a cell phone to school and she would be the only person advocating the other position. This is problematic in terms of numbers and her position as an authority figure. Instead, she decides that the goal of the deliberation will be to determine the two most important reasons that students should be allowed to bring cell phones. Having reviewed the students' work and listened to each presentation, she knows that there are at least five different informed and reasonable positions. While this was not her original intent, it still supports her social studies and critical literacy learning objectives of participating in civil discourse, deliberation, and hearing multiple perspectives. Also recognizing the size of her class, she makes an arrangement with the librarian to supervise one half of her class at a time. Working with just 15 students in the group will allow all of her students to participate in the discussion.

On the afternoon of the deliberation, Mrs. Ramsey follows the same process for each of the two groups. She arranges the students' desks in a circle, sitting in the circle as well. She posts the revised T-Chart and reviews the difference between civil and uncivil discourse. She also suggests that because this is still a large group, even with only one half of the class, students should raise their hands and wait to be called on by her. She reiterates that even though she will be calling on them, their comments should be directed to the entire group, not to her. Mrs. Ramsey then draws the students' attention to the question for the deliberation: *What are the two most important reasons to allow cell phones?* She prompts students to share their refined hypothesis as a starting point, and a few volunteers begin. Mrs. Ramsey models the strategies of building on one another's arguments (e.g., I agree with Sharon that cell phones help us learn, and I have additional evidence from Mr. Schafer, the technology teacher, who has kids use cell phones in his class to give him feedback on understanding), as well as respectfully disagreeing (e.g., I disagree with Sam's position that being able to text your friends is an important reason for cell phones because texting your friends might cause you to not focus on learning). She limits each deliberation to 30 minutes, plenty of time for most students to speak more than once. Across the two groups, the students struggle to reach consensus on the two most important reasons, but are able to support three reasons. While not the original plan, the deliberation allowed the students to engage in discussions, pose questions, and report on a topic in depth, all key goals for fourth graders.

Suggested Resources

There are several online resources available related to the unit. All of the sources were current as of the book's printing but may change over time. You are encouraged to expand on these and continue to seek out additional resources as you plan your unit.

Websites

Bill of Rights

> http://www.archives.gov/exhibits/charters/bill_of_rights.html
> http://billofrightsinstitute.org/founding-documents/bill-of-rights/
> http://www.madisonbrigade.com/library_bor.htm

Federalist and Anti-Federalist Debates

> http://teachingamericanhistory.org/fed-antifed/federalist/

Videos

City Council Meetings

> https://www.youtube.com/watch?v=rFeA-pM0o8Y
> https://www.youtube.com/watch?v=qqOSNI7l0bQ

References

Adler, D. A. & Adler, M. S. (1991). *A picture book of Thomas Jefferson*. New York, NY: Holiday House.

Adler, D. A. & Adler, M. S. (2009). *A picture book of Dolley and James Madison*. New York, NY: Holiday House.

Charles River Editors (2013). *History for kids: The illustrated lives of Founding Fathers–George Washington, Thomas Jefferson, Benjamin Franklin, Alexander Hamilton, and James Madison*. Boston, MA: Author.

Cheney, L. (2010). *We the people: The story of our Constitution*. New York, NY: Simon & Schuster.

Kranich, N. (2010). Promoting adult learning through civil discourse in the public library. *New Directions for Adult and Continuing Education* (127), 15–24.

Lindeman, E. C. L. (1935/1987). The place of discussion in the learning process. Reprinted in S. D. Brookfield, *Learning democracy: Eduard Lindeman on adult education and social change*. Kent, UK: Croom Helm.

Mazurana, D. E. & Bonds, A. E. (2000). A hostile reception: Women's realities of civil political discourse in democracies. *Peace and Conflict: Journal of Peace Psychology*, 6(4), 325–332.

Muth, J. J. (2002). *The three questions*. New York, NY: Scholastic.

Obenchain, K. M. & Morris, R. V. (2015). *50 social studies strategies for K–8 classrooms*. Boston, MA: Pearson.

Parker, W. C. (2001). Classroom discussion: Models for leading seminars and deliberations. *Social Education*, 65(2), 111–115.

Parker, W. C. (2012). *Social studies in elementary education* (14th ed.). Boston, MA: Pearson.

Polacco, P. (1994). *Pink and say*. New York, NY: Philomel Books.

Seixas, P. & Morton, T. (2012). *The big six historical thinking concepts*. Toronto, Canada: Nelson Education.

Sobel, S. (2008). *The Bill of Rights: Protecting our freedom then and now*. Hauppauge, NY: Barron's.

Walmsley, P. (1995). Prince Maurice's rational parrot: Civil discourse in Locke's essay. *Eighteenth-Century Studies*, 28(4), 413–425.

6

WHAT CAN I DO WHEN A LAW IS UNJUST?

A Fifth-Grade Unit on Civil Disobedience

> *I would like to be known as a person who is concerned about freedom and equality and justice and prosperity for all people.*
>
> Rosa Parks

Background Content for Teachers

Civic Concept: Civil Disobedience

Civil disobedience is the deliberate decision and action to publicly and nonviolently protest unjust policies or laws. Civil disobedience, first named by Henry David Thoreau, has been a part of citizens' relationships to laws and responses to power from the nonviolent resistance of Mohandas Gandhi to the response against apartheid. Civil disobedience is done publicly in order to bring attention to, and show clear opposition to, the unjust law (Rawls, 1999). It has been used throughout history and across the globe as individuals and groups have worked for positive change and to end injustice. The famous writer Thoreau protested the Mexican-American War by refusing to pay taxes, recognizing that a portion of his tax dollars would support the war effort. In India, Gandhi utilized civil disobedience in the first half of the twentieth century to protest the British colonial rule that included racist policies in India. Both Thoreau and Gandhi inspired the leaders of the US civil rights movement (CRM) in their work to end legal segregation, among other numerous racist laws and policies. More recently, citizens have been arrested for protesting against what they believe to be unjust laws prohibiting gay marriage, immigration policies, and minimum wage laws. Citizens can use civil disobedience in two ways. One way is to break the unjust law; another way is to break a law while protesting the unjust law. Sometimes citizens break the unjust law to draw attention to the law itself (e.g., Thoreau not paying taxes, Rosa Parks not moving on the bus). In other situations, citizens break another law, such as when and where to protest, because they cannot actually break the unjust law. For example, because citizens who are gay cannot legally get married in many states, they cannot break that law. Instead, some draw attention to the unjust law by violating local protest laws. Clark, Vontz, and Barikmo (2008, p. 52) list four essential features of acts of civil disobedience: (1) the action disobeys a governmental law or policy; (2) the disobedience is deliberate and public; (3) the person who is disobeying the law firmly believes that what he or she is protesting is unjust and that the action of disobeying will bring attention to the unjust law or policy; and (4) disobeying the law must be nonviolent and nondestructive. Thoreau and Gandhi, as well as Martin Luther King, Jr. and other US civil rights leaders and foot soldiers, followed these principles in their work to better society. However, the colonists who participated in the Boston Tea Party did not meet the fourth feature. While they did not hurt anyone, they deliberately destroyed property. For our purposes, we connect civil disobedience to injustice. This allows elementary students to see that civil disobedience is a response to unfair rules.

Historical Content: Rosa Parks and the Civil Rights Movement

In 1955 Rosa Parks became a spark for the national CRM. Often described as a woman who was too tired to give up her seat on the bus in Montgomery, Alabama, after a hard day at work, in reality she was an educated citizen and activist consciously using civil disobedience to change her world. Rosa Parks was educated in social activism at the Highlander Folk School where she participated in workshops led by another civil rights activist, Septima Clark. Mrs. Parks and those who worked for civil rights in the United States knew they needed to take a stand and she became the impetus for escalating the movement by demonstrating the power of not being allowed to sit with Whites on public transportation. She was active in the CRM in Montgomery, Alabama, serving as secretary of the local National Association for the Advancement of Colored People (NAACP) chapter, long before the life-changing bus incident that thrust her from the sidelines occupied by thousands of other foot soldiers to the front lines occupied by a smaller number of courageous citizens. At that time in history, many local communities, particularly those in southern states, had city laws requiring Black citizens to give up their seats on public buses to White citizens. Mrs. Parks was not the first Black woman arrested for refusing to give up her seat, but she was the one tapped by a movement to become the face for the bus boycott. Mrs. Parks's decision to support the lawsuit that challenged Montgomery city bus codes put her and her family in real danger. Rosa Parks's arrest for breaking a law was an example of civil disobedience in that the arrest was the direct result of disobeying an unjust law. Her act altered the course of the CRM in many ways, including catapulting Martin Luther King, Jr. into the national spotlight. But, in relation to civil disobedience, it allowed the movement to illustrate how the Jim Crow laws were unjust. Black citizens nonviolently violated Jim Crow laws and were arrested, all while bringing attention to the laws themselves. The historical event of Rosa Parks's arrest which led to the Montgomery bus boycott, as well as the lunch counter sit-ins in Jackson, Mississippi, and Greensboro, North Carolina, and the various protest marches demonstrate how citizens can alter the course of history by understanding and exercising their civic rights and responsibilities. Rosa Parks spoke against unjust laws; elementary students often talk about what is unfair. While racial segregation and elementary classroom policies are very different in scope, the concept of injustice (unfairness) and citizens' response to the injustice through civil disobedience can be explored conceptually.

Critical Democratic Literacy and Civil Disobedience

Critical Democratic Literacy (CDL) provides a foundation for the larger conceptual goals of our lessons about civil disobedience. At its core, civil disobedience is the informed and purposeful disobeying of laws in order to make the community better for all of the members of the community. Citizens who participate in civil disobedience should also attend to civic virtue and civic engagement, and utilize civil discourse.

Rationale for the Unit

Elementary students need to understand civil disobedience as one type of civic engagement, the civic concept explored in Chapter 4. The elementary social studies curriculum, particularly the civics curriculum, typically focuses on students learning about the importance of communities having laws and obeying laws, as well as the process of making laws. The communities explored vary, but often include the classroom, school, local, state, and national communities. In this sense, a community is a space or place in which we are a member, feel a sense of belonging to, and feel a sense of responsibility to improve. The varied types of communities and the focus on laws is appropriate. However, it is less typical for elementary students to learn about bad or unjust laws and what to do about them. If our goal is to create informed and engaged citizens, they must be informed about what makes a law unjust and how to engage in appropriate ways to bring attention to that injustice. Civic engagement is a requirement of citizens in a democracy, and civil disobedience is one way to do that. Civil disobedience is complex and may even be uncomfortable to teach because it requires students learning that they have the right, and in some situations, the responsibility to break a law. We present this as the last civic concept because civil disobedience should not be examined superficially and without an understanding of civic virtue, civic engagement, and civil discourse.

Chapter Guide

As the chapter moves through a planning session and several lessons, we address the complexity of understanding our students, and the reality that teaching is a recursive process that relies on continuous assessment and revision in response to student and curricular needs. Table 6.1 provides an overview of the unit components and the basic areas addressed across our lessons. Both theory and practice are combined in order to (1) incorporate the theoretical framework of CDL, (2) represent the construction and teaching of lessons focused on social studies and literacy standards, and (3) meet the needs of elementary students. Table 6.1 begins with civil disobedience as the concept to be taught and then moves to an initial assessment using a read-aloud before a more specific unit is designed. The assessment component focuses both on students and on materials in order to adjust instruction based on what the students already know about civil disobedience. As students gain an understanding of the abstract concept of civil disobedience they also use primary source comprehension as they learn facts about the US CRM. This includes information about Martin Luther King, Jr., Rosa Parks, the Montgomery bus boycott, and the bombing of the 16th Avenue Baptist Church in Birmingham, among others. The lessons we present contribute to the larger unit topic of "What can I do when a law is unjust?" The planning then moves through the social studies and literacy objectives for the unit, consisting of multiple lessons, followed by the particular teaching methods used. Finally, the process-planning guide illustrates another assessment of the students and materials as the second lesson is planned. The description of the unit follows Table 6.1.

TABLE 6.1 Process guide for planning a unit on civil disobedience

Civil Disobedience	
Social Studies	*Critical Literacy*
US History	Disrupting the commonplace Taking action and promoting social justice
Initial Assessment	
Students	
What do students know about the concept of civil disobedience? What do they know about the history of the civil rights movement (CRM)?	What do students know about disrupting the commonplace? What do students know about taking action to promote social justice?

	Materials		
Primary source materials related to CRM	*Terrible Things: An Allegory of the Holocaust* *If A Bus Could Talk: The Story of Rosa Parks* *The Story of Ruby Bridges*		

	Standards		
Social Studies Standards (C3 Framework)	Literacy Speaking & Listening Standards (CCSS ELA)	Literacy Reading Standards (CCSS ELA)	Literacy Writing Standards (CCSS ELA)
Civic and Political Institutions: D2.Civ.2.3-5. Explain how a democracy relies on people's responsible participation, and draw implications for how individuals should participate. **Participation and Deliberation: Applying Civic Virtues and Democratic Principles D2.Civ.10.3-5.** Identify the beliefs, experiences, perspectives, and values that underlie their own and others' points of view about civic issues. **Processes, Rules, and Laws: D2.Civ.12.3-5.** Explain how rules and laws change	**Comprehension and Collaboration:** CCSS.ELA-Literacy.SL.5.1 Engage effectively in a range of collaborative discussions (one-on-one, in groups, and teacher-led) with diverse partners on *grade 5 topics and texts*, building on others' ideas and expressing their own clearly. CCSS.ELA-Literacy.SL.5.1.a Come to discussions prepared, having read or studied required material; explicitly draw on that preparation and other	**Key Ideas and Details:** CCSS.ELA-Literacy.RI.5.2 Determine two or more main ideas of a text and explain how they are supported by key details; summarize the text. CCSS.ELA-Literacy.RI.5.3 Explain the relationships or interactions between two or more individuals, events, ideas, or concepts in a historical, scientific, or technical text based on specific information in the text. CCSS.ELA-Literacy.RI.5.5 Compare and contrast the overall structure (e.g., chronology,	**Text Types and Purposes:** CCSS.ELA-Literacy.W.5.1.b Provide logically ordered reasons that are supported by facts and details. CCSS.ELA-Literacy.W.5.3.e Provide a conclusion that follows from the narrated experiences or events. **Production and Distribution of Writing:** CCSS.ELA-Literacy.W.5.4 Produce clear and coherent writing in which the development and organization are appropriate to task, purpose, and audience. (Grade-specific expectations for

(Continued)

TABLE 6.1 Process guide for planning a unit on civil disobedience (*Continued*)

society and how people change rules and laws. **D2.Civ.14.3-5.** Illustrate historical and contemporary means of changing society. **Change, Continuity, and Context:** **D2.His.3.3-5.** Generate questions about individuals and groups who have shaped significant historical changes and continuities. **Historical Sources and Evidence:** **D2.His.10.3-5.** Compare information provided by different historical sources about the past. **D2.His.12.3-5.** Generate questions about multiple historical sources and their relationships to particular historical events and developments. **Causation and Argumentation:** **D2.His.14.3-5.** Explain probable causes and effects of events and developments.	information known about the topic to explore ideas under discussion. CCSS.ELA-Literacy.SL.5.2 Summarize a written text read aloud or information presented in diverse media and formats, including visually, quantitatively, and orally. **Presentation of Knowledge and Ideas:** CCSS.ELA-Literacy.SL.5.5 Include multimedia components (e.g., graphics, sound) and visual displays in presentations when appropriate to enhance the development of main ideas or themes.	comparison, cause/effect, problem/solution) of events, ideas, concepts, or information in two or more texts. CCSS.ELA-Literacy.RI.5.6 Analyze multiple accounts of the same event or topic, noting important similarities and differences in the point of view they represent. **Integration of Knowledge and Ideas:** CCSS.ELA-Literacy.RI.5.7 Draw on information from multiple print or digital sources, demonstrating the ability to locate an answer to a question quickly or to solve a problem efficiently. CCSS.ELA-Literacy.RI.5.9 Integrate information from several texts on the same topic in order to write or speak about the subject knowledgeably.	writing types are defined in standards 1-3 above.) CCSS.ELA-Literacy.W.5.8 Recall relevant information from experiences or gather relevant information from print and digital sources; summarize or paraphrase information in notes and finished work, and provide a list of sources. CCSS.ELA-Literacy.W.5.9 Draw evidence from literary or informational texts to support analysis, reflection, and research.

Learning Objectives Students will:	
Social Studies	Critical Literacy
• Form the concept civil disobedience. • Examine the life of Rosa Parks. Examine and interpret primary source documents and images in their historical context.	• Use texts to describe how disrupting the commonplace has occurred in the past. • Explain how people can take action to promote social justice.

⇩

Instructional Methods	
Social Studies	Critical Literacy
Concept Development Primary Source Comprehension	

⇩

Reassessment of Students & Materials	
Were students able to provide both examples and non-examples of civil disobedience? Were students able to understand primary sources within their historical context?	Were students able to access the literal meaning from the texts? Were students able to compare and contrast the information from the texts?
Revise and reteach as needed, focusing on standards and objectives	

⇩

Revisiting Civil Disobedience: Working Toward Community

Unit Narrative

Our chapter introduces you to the fifth-grade classroom of Ms. Murphy. Ms. Murphy has a bachelor's degree in elementary education and is a 24-year veteran, full-time fifth-grade teacher at Dogwood Elementary. Dogwood has a very diverse student and teacher population. Ms. Murphy's classroom has 29 students. Fifth-grade students' reading and writing abilities are well developed. They should be able to incorporate complex ideas and vocabulary into their speaking and writing as well as read narrative and informational text thoughtfully and critically. Fifth graders are expected to move beyond textual summary and on to evaluation as they are subjected to more content area texts.

Civil Disobedience: Preparing the Lesson

Ms. Murphy plans for a unit on civil disobedience by setting up a learning center on the CRM. The center contains books and historical photographs of the Selma to Montgomery March and the march on Washington, the Montgomery bus boycott, Freedom Rides, lunch counter sit-ins, as well as individuals including Martin Luther King, Jr., Rosa Parks, Dorothy Cotton, JoAnn Robinson, Ralph Abernathy, and John Lewis. She has two goals for this unit of study that focus more on learning concepts and skills than on the memorization of facts. Ms. Murphy recognizes the importance of factual information in understanding concepts. For example, factual knowledge of several CRM events is important to understanding the CRM as something bigger than the "sum of its parts." First, and this is a year-long goal, she wants the students to understand the concept of civil disobedience and connect it to the previous concepts she taught—civic virtue, civic engagement, and civil discourse. The students will need to learn many facts and reflect on their own experiences to understand this concept and how it was a part of the CRM. By using the CRM as a vehicle to teach the concept of civil disobedience, she can use concrete and tangible examples to help students' conceptual understanding (Taba, 1967). Second, she wants the students to continue developing competency in analyzing primary source documents and reading informational texts.

Ms. Murphy wants her students to understand that civil disobedience is when people purposefully break the law to bring attention to unfair laws with the goal of making better laws. She is careful to acknowledge that while her students are studying acts of civil disobedience of the past through the US CRM, acts of civil disobedience are still around today. Her goal is for her students to recognize the CRM's use of civil disobedience as a tool to bring attention to injustice for the purpose of ending it. She also wants her students to recognize issues of injustice they witness and experience in their own lives, and have the skills and dispositions to work toward making their worlds more just. Ms. Murphy prepares her initial assessment of the students, building on what they are already familiar with.

CRITICAL DEMOCRATIC LITERACY

Promoting social justice is the foundation for CDL. Citizens can engage in civic life without considering the others in the larger community. However, CDL highlights the need for a civic identity in which the individual is inherently aware of and connected to their role and positioning in the world.

Initial Assessment

Ms. Murphy uses recent incidents on the playground to assess her students' understandings of justice. There is a new game on the playground called "pest control." In the game certain students are labeled as pests and are then chased around the playground so they can be exterminated. In the game, extermination simply means being touched on the shoulder like in a game of tag. The game has been going on for a few days and being "exterminated" has become a symbol for unpopularity. Ms. Murphy asks the students how they feel about the game. Some students are quiet; others discuss how mean it is. The concept of fairness comes up, and some students state how it is unfair that the same people are always called pests while the others are always the exterminators. Ms. Murphy asks Sarah, "Did one of your friends do something good?" Sarah replies, "Yes, Ana told the kids playing pest control to leave me alone." David, nodding, says, "That was nice of her." Sarah adds, "And she didn't have to, cause she could get chased too. Ben yelled at her and pushed her." Wanting to make the link between the explicit and implicit curriculum very clear and add in the vocabulary word *just*, she then asks the class a series of questions: "Were the kids chasing Sarah and the other students being fair and just? Was Ana, who stood up for Sarah, being fair and just?" Although the terms are abstract, the students begin talking among themselves and offering examples and connections of socially just (and some unjust) behaviors on the playground. The discussion concludes with the students understanding that the pest control game has rules that are unjust. Students' engagement in the discussion clearly requires them to use their listening and speaking skills as they turn to other's perspectives to understand justice.

Ms. Murphy connects this to their ongoing study of fairness and rules. She reminds students that they had discussed how people sometimes do or say things that are good and that will help other people even though it scares them. She also connects these ideas to her previous units on civic virtue, civic engagement, and civil discourse. Her goal is to determine if the students can apply those concepts to the experiences of Ruby Bridges. She then asks, "Can you remember anyone you have been learning about in your civil rights center who did something virtuous for someone else?" Having read biographies on individuals in the CRM, analyzed historical photographs, and watched some news footage, the students offer, "Rosa Parks, Jo Ann Robinson, and Martin Luther King, Jr." Ms. Murphy then asks, "Why were these things virtuous?" Her questions push the students to draw conclusions based on information from texts, media, and images. The students understand that the CRM people were trying to do something good for everyone. In order to address civil disobedience, Ms. Murphy realizes that she must move the students past the idea of just doing something good to the notion of doing something good in the face of obstacles such as fear and laws.

She anticipates that the idea of unjust laws, civil disobedience, as well as how people react violently to acts of civil disobedience may be complex and controversial for elementary students. *The Story of Ruby Bridges* by Robert Coles (1995) focused on realistic paintings of Ruby going to a previously all-White school after the school segregation laws in New Orleans were declared unconstitutional. Participating in the desegregation of her school was very difficult. Ruby knew she was following the law but she was met with angry crowds and had to be protected by the National Guard. These are powerful images and the students need to understand why her seemingly simple act of going to school was a brave and virtuous thing to do in that particular time and place. Gathering the students on the floor in front of her chair, Ms. Murphy begins the story. She describes how Ruby's actions were related to the NAACP's request for volunteers to participate in school integration. Ruby's family responded to the request and sent her to school. After reading the page in Cole's book about Ruby's parents' decision to let Ruby lead the way for other children, Ms. Murphy prompts, "Why would it take strength and courage for Ruby to go to school?" The students share ideas related to being scared to do something that other people may not like. They discuss doing things by themselves and not having friends to back them up. Vasile offers, "They were Black and it was hard to be Black back then." "Yes," Ms. Murphy agrees, "Can anyone give an example of why it was hard to be Black?" Ellie brings up, "The laws were unfair because Black people and White people got to do different things and Black people were sometimes hurt and beat up by bad people." Students also note that Ruby was brave and she did not give up on going to school with the White students.

After the initial assessment, Ms. Murphy observes that making connections and evaluating information is more challenging for her students, but she noticed that they began to understand the concept behind being brave and that not everyone agrees that certain rules or laws are good. This is connected to the earlier discussion of the pest control game where students recognized the unfair rules of the game. She decides that they need some specific connections between fairness and justice as well as challenging an unjust rule or law. Ms. Murphy decides that the students also need to get to the point where they see civil disobedience in the actions of others. This knowledge about the students' experiences and conceptual understandings provides the starting point for planning the unit, beginning with the related standards followed by the instructional objectives and methods.

Standards

Ms. Murphy's unit on civil disobedience focuses on eight standards from the Disciplinary Concepts and Tools section of the C3 Framework (NCSS, 2013). She focuses on four civics standards that explore the creation and changing of rules and four history standards that focus on using historical evidence to help understand the past and the present. While several of the Common Core State Standards for English/Language Arts could apply to the unit, Ms. Murphy elects to hone in on oral language and other standards related to the use of modes such as photos, technology, and texts to research and develop their ideas.

Learning Objectives: "What Can I Do When a Law Is Unjust?"

Civil disobedience is a complex concept for learners of every age. However, as an important social studies concept, and related to democracy, Ms. Murphy

TABLE 6.2 Learning objectives

Students will:	
Social Studies	Critical Literacy
• Form the concept civil disobedience. • Form the concept hero/heroine. • Examine the life of Rosa Parks as one example of a heroine. • Examine and interpret primary source documents and images in their historical context.	• Use texts to describe how disrupting the commonplace has occurred in the past. • Explain how people can take action to promote social justice.

believes it is essential. She wants to be sure that her students understand the risks that individuals and groups in history have taken when participating in civil disobedience, and how informed and thoughtful the historical actors were. She also wants to pursue the nonviolent and law disobedience aspects of the concept. Ms. Murphy decides that examining historical sources (primary sources) is a good next step. Table 6.2 is a reminder of Ms. Murphy's social studies and literacy objectives, which are well-suited to integration. The concepts and individuals that are the subjects of the social studies objectives enacted the critical literacy objectives of disrupting the commonplace and taking action.

Instructional Methods

Ms. Murphy decides to interweave two social studies instructional strategies in the lessons. She is designing concept development and concept attainment lessons, and some of those lessons are going to use historical/primary sources. The concept development instructional strategy was used with kindergartners in Chapter 3 of this book as they learned about civic virtue. Using historical/primary sources in the elementary classroom was first introduced in Chapter 4 of this book as students analyzed a postcard from the women's rights movement. Chapters 3 and 4 contain detailed explanations of these two strategies. In this chapter, Ms. Murphy interweaves these two social studies instructional strategies for her upper elementary students, providing an additional example.

Primary Source Comprehension

Working with the guiding question, "What does it mean to stand up for someone?", Ms. Murphy gathers a variety of resources that will illustrate key components of the concept of civil disobedience. This includes historical and current photographs (e.g., Blacks sitting at a segregated lunch counter, Blacks and Whites sitting next to each other on a public bus, students in a prohibited area of the school yard, a picture of a single protestor in Tiananmen Square, Justin Bieber being arrested for racing on a public street, violent protests against government policies in Ukraine). This combination of historical and current photographs modifies the typical goals of historical source work. Most often, analyzing historical sources is intended to promote historical thinking, a particular type of critical thinking associated with the discipline of history (VanSledright, 2004; Wineburg, 2001) in which students analyze historical documents to better understand the documents, as well as the authors of the documents. In doing so, we can begin to better understand that historical documents were created during particular times and in particular places, they had different purposes (e.g., public, private, governmental, entertainment, propaganda), and that their authors were historical actors. This means that the authors were also situated in particular historical contexts and what they created was representative of that context. This is more evident in some documents than in others and it is important to be aware of the distinction (Barton, 2005). For example, the manifest of a ship that transported enslaved Africans to the Americas was a business document. The author of that document did not create that document as a form of propaganda; his positionality and perspective is less relevant than what the document tells us about how enslaved Africans were identified as property in that particular historical context and by many people. In Ms. Murphy's lesson using both historical and current sources, she is looking to help students develop conceptual knowledge of the civic concept of civil disobedience. The sourcing heuristic she uses may be used to frame document-based questions to promote historical thinking; however, her questions are not historically grounded. Sourcing is also connected to the literacy skill of summarizing information from a diverse range of media and developing students' ability to draw on information from multiple print and media sources.

Ms. Murphy gathers photographs that illustrate examples and non-examples of civil disobedience during the CRM and the Ukrainian uprising. In choosing appropriate photographs, she realizes that students will need to explore two separate dimensions, or essential characteristics, of civil disobedience. Working from the definition of civil disobedience as the deliberate decision and action to protest unjust policies or laws through the nonviolent disobedience of laws, she separates the disobedience of unjust laws from nonviolent action or protest. She wants students to distinguish between unjust and just laws, as well as distinguish between nonviolent and violent protests. This portion of the lesson focuses on concept attainment (Taba, 1967) in that Ms. Murphy is working from an existing definition of civil disobedience. Her students are not building the definition; they are examining a variety of examples that could be civil disobedience in order to determine if they are examples or non-examples. This will assist students in deepening their understanding of the concept by applying it to new examples. Ms. Murphy also wants the students to gain experience in analyzing historical/primary sources and to utilize oral language—this goal drives the first set of activities. She realizes that building this important, but complex, conceptual understanding will require several different activities. After making four sets of the photographs, she divides the class into four heterogeneous working groups, giving each group one set of photographs and a set of questions that facilitate various levels of source analysis. For this lesson, she follows a three-step primary source analysis procedure (sourcing heuristic) (Obenchain & Morris, 2015).

Literal Primary Source Comprehension

For each photograph, students are asked to complete a literal description of the source. Building on both social studies and literacy, literal description is similar to literal comprehension. That is, students are not asked to interpret the source. Rather, they are asked to describe what they see and read in order to establish a clear understanding of the source prior to any more in-depth analysis. This includes a description of what is going on in the photograph, who is in the photograph, and a description of all of the details (e.g., black-and-white or color, background, text).

One of the black-and-white photographs that she includes was taken by Fred Blackwell. The photograph is from a 1963 Woolworth's lunch counter sit-in in Jackson, Mississippi. The photograph shows several Black and White individuals seated at the lunch counter. There is a large crowd of Whites standing behind them, and at least one person is pouring a large glass of what appears to be a milkshake onto the head of one of the people seated. This photograph, like many from the civil rights era, is accessible through the Internet from reputable sites like libraries, the National Archives and Records Administration, and the Library of Congress. Ms. Murphy circles the student groups discussing their photos and hears various comments. Regarding the lunch counter sit-in photograph, students offer "there are Black and White people sitting at a counter," "this looks like a restaurant," "there are White people standing up behind the Black people," and "some White people are pouring stuff on the Black people's heads." One student states, "They are so mean!" As she moves from group to group, she reminds them to simply describe first and save their interpretations and evaluations for the next set of questions. It is important to reinforce this skill, encouraging students to "see" or "hear" everything in the source.

Interpretive Primary Source Comprehension

After students have thoroughly described each photograph, Ms. Murphy asks the groups to interpret the photographs with prompts and questions that support the concept development of civil disobedience. This illustrates Ms. Murphy's modification of typical historical/primary source work. While her students are being asked document-based questions, the questions are not always connected to historical thinking. Students are directed to talk about what they believe is going on in the photograph. She provides a few guiding questions to facilitate the interpretation such as: "Describe what the people are doing. Why are the people just sitting there while food is poured on them? Are they all doing the same thing or different things? How do you believe the people feel? Who do you think took the photograph? Why do you believe it was taken? Does the photograph seem recent or older? Is anyone hurting anyone?" Students must provide evidence from the photographs for their interpretations. For the lunch counter sit-in, students state that the people sitting at the counter do not appear to be reacting to getting things poured on their heads. They also note that some of the people doing the pouring are smiling but none of the people sitting at the counter are smiling. From this observation, students interpret and infer that the people sitting at the counter were not happy; some students also note that the Black woman looks sad.

Evaluative Primary Source Comprehension

Before the next level of analysis, Ms. Murphy reads *Terrible Things: An Allegory of the Holocaust* by Eve Bunting. The book provides a clear example of what can happen when we do not stand up for others when something terrible or unfair happens. The consequences of standing by and watching as others are treated badly are that injustice spreads unchecked, hurting everyone. As the students listen to the story of how the terrible things come to the forest for every animal with feathers, and then for others, the white rabbits do not speak up. Finally, the rabbits are targeted and the terrible things come for them. This illustrates how since the rabbits did not stand up for the other animals, they allowed the terrible things to continue to take all of the animals and the terrible things eventually came for the rabbits. The book leads the students into a discussion of what the animals could have done to protect and help each other. She also asks the students to use their knowledge of point of view to try to understand the various animals' points of view and perspectives. As the students share ideas from "they could have beat them up" to "they could have all hidden," she slowly weaves the term, "standing up for others" into the students' ideas and writes the term on the board. She presents the idea that the animals could have organized and become a group larger than the terrible things to protect each other and change things.

Next, Ms. Murphy asks the small groups to evaluate the actions taken by individuals in the photographs using the idea of standing up for yourself and others, and to consider what they could learn from those actions. Reminding the students that they are studying the CRM, she asks the students to consider how these photographs help them to understand more about the CRM and other movements for civil rights. She also asks them how these photographs create more questions about other social movements. Building on their interpretations and *Terrible Things*, students mention, "They are not helping each other; they are just sitting there." In relation to the Ukraine photo, the students comment on the man fighting the officers and see him as standing up for himself. Due to the variety of the photos, the conversations vary and finally Ms. Murphy brings the students together to broaden the conversation. Students begin to connect the ideas, stating, "We should know that you should not let people be mean to you," "you should help your friends," and "I don't want to stand up for someone if I could get in trouble." She notes that the students are applying the idea of standing up for someone, but they are still not specifically talking about fair or just reasons or differentiating between violent and nonviolent protesting.

> **CRITICAL DEMOCRATIC LITERACY**
>
> CDL is reliant on understanding the importance of virtuous collective action. It is crucial that citizens must work together on behalf of others to recognize, respond, and ultimately end injustice for all.

Concept Attainment

The next day, and after the students thoroughly examined the photographs, Ms. Murphy moves on to the concept attainment portion of the concept lesson. The photographs are again distributed to four heterogeneous working groups. The student groups are directed to separate the photographs into two groups: (1) photos of people standing up to benefit themselves and others, but doing so violently, and (2) photos of people standing up to benefit themselves and others, and who remain nonviolent. As Ms. Murphy moves around the room, facilitating each student group, she reminds the students to draw on their prior knowledge of civil rights movements and the *Terrible Things* book for some of the pictures. By doing so, she is pushing her students to rely on their knowledge, not just their emotional responses. Once the groups are done, they present their analysis to the class by posting their pictures on a class wall chart with the headers "standing up violently" and "standing up nonviolently." At this point in the lesson Ms. Murphy has not connected standing up for someone to specifically breaking a law to do so. This will be the last part of the definition, as well as the most abstract, for her students to learn.

Evaluation

After completing their presentations to the entire class, Ms. Murphy steps in to develop a class definition of both violently and nonviolently standing up for others. The students return to their small groups to discuss and write down their ideas, relying primarily on the pictures and their personal experiences. Each group produces a three-sentence definition of how and why to stand up for others. Statements such as, "Standing up for someone means that you risk your life to keep them safe. You watch out for them. You make sure they are not bullied." Others construct definitions such as, "You have to fight for your friends," and "Sometimes you have to be brave." Ms. Murphy places the definitions on the class chart as the students share their work, reading aloud to the class.

TABLE 6.3 Civil disobedience definition

Civil disobedience is:
1. standing up for the rights of others
2. when laws are unjust
3. without hurting anyone

Knowing that it is time to connect these ideas to the larger concept of civil disobedience, Ms. Murphy reads the book *If a Bus Could Talk: The Story of Rosa Parks* (Ringold, 2003). During and after the reading, she draws the students' attention to why Rosa Parks chose to break the law by not relinquishing her seat. Ms. Murphy directly states that Parks broke the law. She reminds them of what the Jim Crow laws were. She then connects the actions of Parks to the student definitions of standing up for someone and brings their attention to Parks's nonviolent act that helped begin the bus boycott. She discusses the unjust Jim Crow laws and how Mrs. Parks was also standing up for others who were not allowed to sit in the front of the bus. Finally, Ms. Murphy introduces the term *civil disobedience* and applies it to Parks. She writes the new definition of standing up for someone without being violent (civil disobedience) on a poster board (Table 6.3) and displays it at the front of the room so they can use it evaluate new examples as they continue to learn.

To continue her goal of conceptual understanding of the civic concept of civil disobedience, Ms. Murphy also shares a definition of civil disobedience from the Merriam-Webster online dictionary that states: "refusal to obey governmental demands or commands especially as a nonviolent and usually collective means of forcing concessions from the government" (http://www.merriam-webster.com/dictionary/civil%20disobedience, accessed September 23, 2014). Ms. Murphy asks the students to compare and contrast the definitions to reinforce the essential elements of justice and nonviolence. The students note that both definitions include nonviolence, but that the Merriam-Webster definition includes the words "refusal to obey," a difference from their class definition. Ms. Murphy asks the students to talk with a partner about why "refusal to obey" might be present. After a brief time for discussion, one pair offers that refusing to obey a law is important because, like they learned in *If A Bus Could Talk*, refusing to obey unjust laws is not easy, but it is important in order to stand up for others and make the community better for everyone. Another pair agrees and brings in what they learned from the photograph of the lunch counter sit-ins where Blacks broke the unjust Jim Crow law. They explained that it would be very difficult and dangerous for just one person to eat at a segregated lunch counter, while another student offers, "And maybe if you did it by yourself, you might be scared or no one would notice and it might not change a lot of things. If more people work on a problem, you help each other and more people know about it." Based on this new information, Ms. Murphy edits the class definition of civil disobedience (Table 6.4) and encourages the students to continue to think about what changes need to be made in the definition before they continue their study.

TABLE 6.4 Civil disobedience definition (revised)

Civil disobedience is:
1. standing up for the rights of others
2. when laws are unjust
3. without hurting anyone
4. disobeying an unjust law

Reassessment of Students and Materials

Ms. Murphy noted that the students understood the difference between violent and nonviolent and standing up to injustice through analyzing a variety of primary sources, texts, and critical discussions; however, the students are still having some difficulty in understanding the broader concept of civil disobedience because it can be complicated. For example, civil disobedience can be enacted by a group or an individual. It has to be a nonviolent protest, but the response may still be violent. Finally, it includes breaking a law, but sometimes an action can be disobedient in one situation but not another. For example, not every protest march violates a law. In the Rosa Parks situation, if the front section of the bus had not filled up with White passengers, Mrs. Parks's seat would not have been in the White section. It was only when the front filled that Mrs. Parks was asked to move further back, and then she refused: this was when she violated a Montgomery city law. Ms. Murphy decides to ask students to connect Rosa Parks to the earlier story of Ruby Bridges, so they can determine if their actions would fall under the class definition of civil disobedience. She reviews the two books and then leads the class in a discussion about their actions. She assists the students in understanding that Ruby did meet the first three criteria but not the fourth, in that she did not disobey an unjust law, while Parks's decision to stay in her seat did meet all four of the criteria. Now that the students are able to evaluate actions using the class definition, Ms. Murphy decides to add one more activity to provide the students with an opportunity to both evaluate acts and create visual representation of their analysis using the revised class definition of civil disobedience (Table 6.4). She again uses the concept attainment model (Taba, 1967), which further advances the learning of a concept by examining examples and non-examples of the larger concept. Civil disobedience is a difficult concept for elementary students, and Ms. Murphy provides multiple and varied opportunities for her students to construct and examine the concept. She has introduced individual essential elements of the concept, building each one before adding new essential elements. Fifth graders are required to draw evidence from various sources in order to analyze and report on topics. The time spent on bringing the students into a deeper understanding of civil disobedience allows students to immerse themselves in the idea of what the concept means across situations. In particular, Ms. Murphy is looking to see if students can discern examples vs. non-examples of the concept of civil disobedience. She asks them to find historical events and current events

TABLE 6.5 Selma to Montgomery March at Edmund Pettus Bridge

Students chose an historical photograph pulled from the National Archives and Records Administration website. The photograph is of marchers in the background and police in the foreground at the Edmund Pettus Bridge.	Students chose an historical photograph pulled from the National Archives and Records Administration website. The photograph is of one police officer raising a club as if to strike marcher who is on his knees and one arm on the back of his head. Other police officers in gas masks are in the background.
Selma to Montgomery March	*Selma to Montgomery March Response*
The freedom marchers are marching across bridge singing on their way to the Alabama state capitol. They wanted to be able to vote.	Armed officers attacked them. They did not fight back. They were standing up for their right to vote. They helped the voting rights movement.
Our Evaluation of the Selma to Montgomery March The marchers are marching and they are not hurting people even though they are being hurt.	
These are examples of civil disobedience because:	
1. The Black people are standing up for the rights of other Black people. 2. They know the laws keeping them from voting are unjust. 3. They walked without hurting anyone. 4. They disobeyed the unjust law against marching in Alabama.	

that demonstrate civil disobedience examples and non-examples. Knowing that this may be difficult for students, she creates specific topics and materials for them to pursue and select to ensure that the materials are appropriate for their age and abilities. This is crucial in assessing whether students have attained conceptual understanding. For example, one group analyzes two photographs taken at the Edmund Pettus Bridge during the Selma to Montgomery March (Table 6.5).

Their work demonstrates their basic understanding of civil disobedience and the CRM. Feeling comfortable with this level of understanding and analysis, Ms. Murphy then moves on to current events to check students' understanding of the concept of civil disobedience by sharing more recent events in Ukraine. Students construct a storyboard about public protests in Ukraine (Table 6.6). She continues to bring in historical narratives, literature, and other resources to provide multiple opportunities for students to use their CDL knowledge as an analytical tool to understand their world.

The students began to see the complexity of evaluating acts of civil disobedience as they looked at the events in Ukraine as a new example. They used the class definition and continued to have questions. Ms. Murphy used this opportunity to explain how complicated civil disobedience is, in part, because laws vary

What Can I Do When a Law is Unjust? 123

TABLE 6.6 Protests in Ukraine

Students chose an Associated Press photograph pulled from the Internet. The photograph shows police wearing riot gear with raised clubs moving toward unarmed and non-resisting protestors.	Students chose an Associated Press photograph pulled from the Internet. The photograph shows a police line with police wearing riot gear standing and facing protestors. One protestor is at the line and spraying something toward the police.
Ukraine Protest	*Ukraine Protest Response*
The protestors in Ukraine are standing up to their government. They do not like that their government wants to do more things with Russia. The protestors are being attacked by soldiers.	This protestor is spraying something at the soldiers. This could hurt the soldiers so it is violent.
Our Evaluation of the Protests in Ukraine In Ukraine, protestors are standing up for one another, but the protests are sometimes violent.	
These **may** be examples of civil disobedience because:	
1. They are standing up for the rights of others by protesting. 2. They believe the laws may become unjust if Ukraine combines with Russia. 3. Some people protested without hurting anyone BUT some people were protesting violently. 4. They may or may not be disobeying an unjust law.	

across countries, states, neighborhoods, and cities. Ms. Murphy then evaluates the students and finds that most of them are able to discern the differences between examples and non-examples of civil disobedience. As the students share their work, she questions them and requires them to use the definition to defend their evaluations. Satisfied with their work, she then moves to a more complex mode of analysis and production.

Revisiting Civil Disobedience: Moving Toward Community

The final activity involves having the students write and compose digital stories of their understandings of how civil disobedience is related to the CRM. Using the class definition as a foundation, as well as additional photographs and videos of the sit-ins, the marches, and the bus boycott, Ms. Murphy asks the students to create a digital story based on what civil disobedience looked like in the past and what it looks like today. Digital stories provide the students with the opportunity to explore various media as well as evaluate their sources and presentation components. Digital stories have various structures and modes. For her class Ms. Murphy has students use their iPads to save images, video clips, and voice-overs. Students prepare storyboards using historical photographs, adding relevant text explaining the photos in relation to civil disobedience with a focus on the four parts of the class definition of civil disobedience.

Over the next few days, the groups work to develop their storyboards and then begin to create scripts using and citing their sources. After revisions and editing sessions where groups evaluated each other's work, the digital stories are previewed to the class before they are shared with other classes in the school. Bringing the information, via the digital stories, to other classrooms requires the students to not only share their work, but also to introduce their topics and respond to questions from their peers in other rooms. The sense of audience and appropriateness of the presentation is critical to the writing process and focuses students' attention on the necessity of relying on sources for outside audiences. Ms. Murphy continues to add in additional assessments related to reading and analyzing other primary sources, and evaluating the perspective of their social studies textbook. We end our chapter, but this is not the end for Ms. Murphy. Her teaching is a constantly recursive process and will continue throughout the school year as they bring the concept of civil disobedience into their study of other historical events, current events, and informational texts.

Suggested Resources

John F. Kennedy Presidential Library (http://www.jfklibrary.org/JFK/JFK-in-History/Civil-Rights-Movement.aspx)

National Park Service (http://www.cr.nps.gov/nr/travel/civilrights/)

PBS (http://www.pbs.org/wnet/aaworld/timeline/civil_01.html)

The Gilda Leherman Institute for American History (http://www.gilderlehrman.org/history-now/2006-06/civil-rights-movement)

The Library of Congress (www.loc.gov)

The National Archives and Records Administration (www.archives.gov)

The Texas Politics Project: Civil disobedience and non-violent action (http://texaspolitics.utexas.edu/archive/html/ig/features/0607_01/slide1.html)

References

Barton, K. C. (2005). Primary sources in history: Breaking through the myths. *Phi Delta Kappan*, 86, 745–753.

Bunting, E. (1989). *Terrible things: An allegory of the Holocaust*. Philadelphia, PA: The Jewish Publication Society.

Clark, J. S., Vontz, T. S., & Barikmo, K. (2008). Teaching about civil disobedience: Clarifying a recurring theme in the secondary social studies. *Social Studies*, 99(2), 51–56.

Coles, R. (1995). *The story of Ruby Bridges*. New York, NY: Scholastic Paperbacks.

National Center for History in the Schools. (1996). *National standards for history*. Los Angeles, CA: Author.

National Council for the Social Studies. (1994). *Expectations of excellence: Curriculum standards for social studies*. Washington, DC: Author.

Rawls, J. (1999). *A theory of justice*. Cambridge, MA: Harvard University Press.

Ringold, F. (2003). *If a bus could talk: The story of Rosa Parks*. New York, NY: Aladdin Paperbacks.

Taba, H. (1967). *Teacher's handbook for elementary social studies*. New York, NY: Addison-Wesley.

VanSledright, B. A. (2004). What does it mean to think historically…and how do you teach it? *Social Education, 68*(3), 230–233.

Wineburg, S. (2001). *Historical thinking and other unnatural acts: Charting the future of teaching the past*. Philadelphia, PA: Temple University Press.

PART III
Implementing Critical Democratic Literacy

7
CRITICAL DEMOCRATIC LITERACY
Key Concepts and Pedagogy

Critical Democratic Literacy (CDL) in the classroom relies on teacher knowledge. This chapter is designed to provide you with additional conceptual knowledge and related curricular ideas to help you plan your own units. While the lessons provided in Chapters 3–6 illustrate the various aspects of teaching CDL using specific classroom examples, this chapter can be used as one reference for building lessons from your own curriculum requirements.

Four Guiding Civic Concepts for Critical Democratic Literacy

As a field, social studies is full of abstract concepts that students struggle to learn because of the complexity of the concepts, as well as the developmental levels of students. Political science concepts such as democracy, rules, and authority; economic concepts such as supply and demand and scarcity; geographic concepts such as environments and patterns; and historical concepts such as chronology and cause and effect should be taught and reviewed frequently in order to move students from learning discrete and seemingly unrelated facts to a deeper understanding of the concepts and the discipline (Brophy & Alleman, 2008; Downey & Levstik, 1998; Scheurman, 2012). As you read through the previous four chapters, you also saw the necessity of slowly and deliberately building that conceptual knowledge. The four interrelated civics-related concepts—civic virtue, civic engagement, civil discourse, and civil disobedience—explored in this book are essential in the education of citizens who are critically and democratically literate. The careful integration of these concepts to address both the social studies and literacy curricula creates the opportunity for deeper and contextualized learning. In the following section, each of the four concepts you were introduced to in Chapters 3–6 are more fully defined. In addition, we included additional ideas for teaching these concepts throughout the K–6 curriculum. You will notice that many of the additional ideas provided cut across the four concepts, just as the four civic concepts cross the K–6 curriculum. These are large and complex ideas and learning them requires multiple, meaningful, and integrative experiences.

Civic Virtue

In its most simple form, civic virtue consists of the personal qualities necessary to commit to live life as a good citizen for one's own benefit, and, just as importantly, the good of the community (Dagger, 1997; Galston, 2007; Merry, 2012). These qualities may be expressed as a disposition to behave in certain ways that are beneficial to the community. One civic virtue might be the disposition and ability to engage in civil discourse with others, especially those who believe differently, with the goal of, at minimum, a deeper understanding of an issue (Jefferson et al., 2014). Another civic virtue might be the valuing of diverse perspectives, recognizing that the knowledge and experiences of others, while different and possibly contradictory to our own knowledge and experiences, has the potential to enlighten all of us and improve our communities.

In the United States, civic virtue is built on two major political philosophies, civic republicanism and traditional liberalism. Civic virtue is often discussed as part of a political philosophy called *civic republicanism* (Pettit, 1997), which requires that citizens set aside their personal interests and individual rights for the good of, and preservation of, the broader political community. In some cases, this might even mean acting in ways that may not be seen as personally advantageous. However, civic republicans believe that, overall, acting for the good of the community, often called the common or public good, will be personally beneficial. In summary, an individual's personal fulfillment is dependent on a politically healthy common good. In addition, in the United States, civic virtue is also influenced by the political philosophy of traditional liberalism, which prioritizes the protection of the individual rights of citizens (Quigley & Bahmueller, 1991) before that of the common good. From this perspective, the best way to have a politically healthy democracy is to first ensure that individual rights are secured. In the United States, we have the challenge of prioritizing both philosophies in our efforts to strengthen the common good (classic republicanism) with efforts to preserve individual rights (traditional liberalism) in our unique vision of civic virtue. While civic virtue is often discussed at a national level, some scholars (e.g., Merry) argue that civic virtue is present and important at the neighborhood and local community level and does not need to be political (e.g., voting). Galston (2007) disagrees, believing that civic virtue does require a political dimension. He suggests that someone can be a good or virtuous person, but not necessarily a good or virtuous citizen, if he does not contribute to the good of the political community. There is an additional dimension here as well. Citizens who support a government or political system that promotes injustice are not exhibiting civic virtue. They may be active in promoting a common cause, but an unjust cause does not benefit the political and civic community. Citizens display civic virtue when they fight injustice through all of the judicial and legislative ways possible, but do not violate the law. Working to end injustice benefits the common good and it protects individual rights. In the United States, this still leaves us with some things to question. What about civil disobedience? Civil disobedience (the fourth concept explored later in this chapter) is a nonviolent breaking of the law that may seem to contradict civic virtue as it can disrupt society. The men and women who peacefully violated Birmingham's city segregation laws were consciously breaking an unjust law. These citizens were not supporting Birmingham's political community and were actively working to change the status quo. Few of us would believe that their decisions were not civically virtuous. Their courageous confrontation of institutional injustice promoted their individual rights, the rights of others, and a healthier democracy. (See Table 7.1.)

TABLE 7.1 Civic virtue across the elementary grades: Additional ideas for lessons on civic virtue

Civic Concept	Grade Level	Typical Social Studies Scope and Sequence	CDL Content Guiding Questions	Relevant Civics and History Content Examples
Civic Virtue	K*	Self	Who are some examples of people in the past and present doing good things for others? Why is going to school part of being a good citizen?	Malala Yousafzai, Jane Addams and Hull House
	1	School and Family	How do citizens balance their personal and civic responsibilities?	George Washington as the American "Cincinnatus"
	2	Neighborhoods	How do members of our communities make life better for everyone in the community?	Community political and civic leaders; local issues like homelessness, hunger, use of public spaces, etc.

(*Continued*)

TABLE 7.1 Civic virtue across the elementary grades: Additional ideas for lessons on civic virtue (*Continued*)

Civic Concept	Grade Level	Typical Social Studies Scope and Sequence	CDL Content Guiding Questions	Relevant Civics and History Content Examples
Civic Virtue	3	Communities Near and Far	What roles did people of various backgrounds, experiences, and perspectives contribute to the founding and development of our community? Who are some important community leaders in different countries that we can learn about civic virtue from?	Community census records and newspapers; early local community leaders, international community leaders such as Wangari Maathai (Kenya), Liu Xiaobo (China), Nelson Mandela (South Africa)
	4	State and Region	What contributions have our state's residents made to benefit the nation?	Political and civic leaders from each state; important Supreme Court cases that originated in each state
	5	US History	How did the founders and framers of the early US exhibit civic virtue in the institutions and documents they created? When and how have our political and civic institutions fallen short of the ideal of civic virtue and how did we, or are we, working to fix those institutions?	Founding Fathers, Declaration of Independence, US Constitution; comparing Plessy v. Ferguson to Brown v. Board of Education of Topeka, KS
	6	Beyond the United States	How do people from different nations work together in positive ways?	United Nations, Doctors without Borders, and other NGOs; peace treaties

*The shaded row indicates the lessons fully developed in Chapter 3 of this book.

Civic Engagement

Civic engagement is the individual or collective actions that people take to make their communities better. This includes one person's volunteerism at a local spay/neuter clinic to reduce pet overpopulation in the community, the youth uprising in Egypt that demanded an improved political and economic state, and voting in political elections. Civic engagement is best experienced and more powerful when citizens join together to work toward a goal. Even when one person volunteers at the animal shelter or participates in a political protest, each person is engaging in a system, even if they are engaging in different actions (e.g., bathing pets, facilitating pet adoptions), and sometimes engaging in the same action (e.g., marching together). Some scholars distinguish between *political engagement* (affecting public policy and government institutions, including working for causes and candidates, and voting) and *civic engagement* (making the community better through community and issue volunteerism) (Wicks, Wicks, Morimoto, Maxwell, & Schulte, 2014), although it is clear that these types of engagement overlap. For example, members of a community may want to make a local park safer and more inviting for the community. This could include political participation through speaking at relevant public meetings, campaigning for council members who support the initiative, voting to support the city's purchase of the park, and supporting any needed financial support through taxation, including police patrols, lighting, and grounds maintenance. In addition, citizens engage in civic participation by organizing a park clean-up, approaching businesses to donate playground equipment, and becoming part of a neighborhood watch in the park's immediate area. In this book, and for our purposes, we use the term *civic engagement* as an umbrella term to encompass all of those ways citizens engage in their communities to make them better. Making a community better illustrates the importance of civically engaging with civic virtue. What may be better for one community member may not be better for all members of the community or the community as a whole. Considering civic virtue and civic engagement together requires that citizens carefully reflect upon the good of the community, as well as their own civic interests as they engage (see Table 7.2). Democracy, as a political system, requires its citizens to engage in the civic and political lives of their communities. In other words, civic engagement is a civic responsibility. Young people's civic engagement is "positively related to knowledge of political systems, pro-social behavior, social responsibility, and future civic engagement" (Hart, Donnelly, Youniss, & Atkins, 2007; Hart & Gullan, 2010; Reinders & Youniss, 2006; Schmid, 2012, as cited in Hope & Jagers, 2014). In other words, students who learn about civic engagement and becoming engaged in civic life as students, particularly during adolescence, are also engaged in civic life as adults.

TABLE 7.2 Civic engagement across the elementary grades: Additional ideas for lessons on civic engagement

Civic Concept	Grade Level	Typical Social Studies Scope and Sequence	CDL Content Guiding Questions	Relevant Disciplinary Content
Civic Engagement	K	Self	Who are people in history who can teach me about civic engagement?	Benjamin Franklin, Abigail Adams, Martin Luther King, Jr., Malcolm X
	1	School and Family	How do we engage in our classroom and school community individually and collectively?	Creating rules, service-learning (tying the academic curriculum to a civic cause/issue)
	2	Neighborhoods	How do we work together in our various communities to make our communities better for everyone?	Caesar Chavez and Dolores Huerta; Farm Workers' Movement
	3★	Communities Near and Far	How can citizens become civically engaged if they cannot vote?	US women's rights movement, Lucretia Mott, Elizabeth Cady Stanton
	4	State and Region	How are elections a form of civic engagement? How do we elect our leaders?	Local, state, and national elections procedures; electoral requirements
	5	US History	What are major social movements in US History?	US women's rights movement, civil rights movement, Labor Movement, Farm Workers' Movement
	6	Beyond the United States	How does civic engagement differ for citizens living in various types of political systems?	Mexico, Canada, China, Japan, Denmark, Russia, Syria, Israel, India, etc.

★The shaded row indicates the lessons fully developed in Chapter 4 of this book.

Civil Discourse

Civil discourse may be one of the earliest examples of what good citizens in a democratic state do; citizens talk about matters of importance. Civil discourse can be defined as learning through discussing (Kranich, 2010; Lindemann, 1935). It requires that citizens who are well informed and rational participate in thoughtful and meaningful conversations with one another to more deeply understand public issues and often to make decisions that affect community. A familiar example might be the New England town meeting in which all members of the community met to discuss issues and concerns relevant to the town or political community. This may include accepting or rejecting the town's budget, hiring and firing of town officials, examining zoning requests, etc. According to philosopher John Locke, what makes civil discourse different from other forms of discussion is the focus on public or civic issues (Walmsley, 1995). In order to move toward understanding any issue, citizens must engage in discussions with those who believe both similarly and differently from one another. It is easy to participate in discussions about an issue when we share similar beliefs about the issue, even if we bring different knowledge to the discussion. However, civil discourse requires engaging with those who believe differently from us. That engagement is often uncomfortable and unsettling, and may challenge our core beliefs, but we will learn more and arrive at a deeper understanding (see Table 7.3). In other words, we cannot learn if we are not uncomfortable. Civil discourse requires that we enter those discussions knowledgeable, open to new knowledge, and with reason. Engaging in civil discourse can be done orally and face-to-face, in writing, through visual representation, and online. While all of these forms required knowledge and reason, the different forms of discussion may require different skills. A potential benefit to some alternative forms of civil discourse (i.e., not face-to-face) is that the additional forms may mitigate existing power relationships that could affect equitable participation in the discussion. These power differentials vary, but could include age, gender, race, ability, and the language of the discussion. Teachers will need to work carefully on the development of skills and dispositions so that every student who enters the discussion as an informed participant is able to engage in the discussion.

TABLE 7.3 Civil discourse across the elementary grades: Additional ideas for lessons on civil discourse

Civic Concept	Grade Level	Typical Social Studies Scope and Sequence	CDL Content Guiding Questions	Relevant Disciplinary Content
Civil Discourse	K	Self	How can I use facts to support what I know?	Why we/class/school, etc., have rules

(*Continued*)

TABLE 7.3 Civil discourse across the elementary grades: Additional ideas for lessons on civil discourse (*Continued*)

Civic Concept	Grade Level	Typical Social Studies Scope and Sequence	CDL Content Guiding Questions	Relevant Disciplinary Content
Civil Discourse	1	School and Family	How do we discuss important issues with one another respectfully in the classroom?	Weekly classroom meetings, deliberations
	2	Neighborhoods	How do our local political and civic leaders make decisions for the good of all of us?	Community, town, and city council meetings
	3	Communities Near and Far	What are the important issues candidates are discussing? In what ways are they engaging in civil discourse? How do we let candidates know our views?	Candidate debates, letters to the editor
	4★	State and Region	How did the Founders and Framers resolve their disagreements?	James Madison and Thomas Jefferson; Declaration of Independence; Federalists and Anti-Federalists
	5	US History	What have been the most important public and civic issues that Americans have disagreed on throughout history? How was civil discourse used in addressing these issues?	Constitutional amendments, including 13th, 14th, 15th, and 20th; Civil War, anti-war protests, immigration policies
	6	Beyond the United States	What are the most important public issues that nations around the world are discussing? How are these issues similar to and different from issues under discussion in the United States?	Fair elections, educational access, clean water, health care access

★The shaded row indicates the lessons fully developed in Chapter 5 of this book.

Civil Disobedience

Civil disobedience has been defined as the public, nonviolent, and conscious violation of the law, specifically for the purpose of showing one's opposition to the law (Rawls, 1999). In addition, by knowingly breaking the law, a person takes responsibility for his or her actions and accepts the legal punishment, even if that includes imprisonment (Quigley & Bahmueller, 1991). This acceptance of legal consequences, even if those consequences are unjust, has been seen in the jailing of civil rights activists, anti-nuclear energy protestors, and anti-war activists, among others. Both words in the term are key in understanding civil disobedience. *Civil* relates to a respect for civil society and civic life, while *disobedience* is an acknowledgement that a protestor is disobeying authority by breaking a law. The power in civil disobedience is that in nonviolently violating the law, the unjust nature of the law is exposed, which also means that disobeying the law occurs publicly and with a clear civic or political purpose. While civic virtue is often seen as having its roots in the civic republican political tradition that advocates the protection of the common good, civil disobedience may be seen as having its roots in political liberalism and the protection of individual rights (Smith, 2011). It has been used throughout history and across the globe as individuals and groups have worked for positive change and to end injustice. (See Table 7.4.) As mentioned in Chapter 6, Henry David Thoreau protested the Mexican-American War by refusing to pay taxes, recognizing that a portion of his tax dollars would support the war effort. Refusing to pay taxes is a violation of the law, but it allowed Thoreau, a well-known writer, to bring attention to what he thought was an unjust war and a misuse of American tax dollars. In India, Mohandas Gandhi, a British-educated lawyer, utilized civil disobedience to protest the British colonial rule that included racist policies in India. Indian independence was his primary goal and he pursued this through a particular type of civil disobedience often called non-cooperation. Through this nonviolent method of boycotting, illegal marching, and the protestation of unfair taxes, Gandhi and his colleagues eventually gained independence for India. Both Thoreau and Gandhi inspired the leaders of the US civil rights movement in their work to end legal segregation, among other numerous racist laws and policies. Clark, Vontz, and Barikmo (2008, p. 52) list four essential features of acts of civil disobedience: (1) The action disobeys a governmental law or policy; (2) the disobedience is deliberate and public; (3) the person who is disobeying the law firmly believes that what he or she is protesting is unjust and that the action of disobeying will bring attention to the unjust law or policy; and (4) disobeying the law must be nonviolent. Thoreau and Gandhi, as well as Martin Luther King, Jr. and other US civil rights leaders and foot soldiers, followed these principles in their work to better society.

TABLE 7.4 Civil disobedience across the elementary grades: Additional ideas for lessons on civil disobedience

Civic Concept	Grade Level	Typical Social Studies Scope and Sequence	CDL Content Guiding Questions	Relevant Disciplinary Content
Civil Disobedience	K	Self	Is it ever okay to break a rule or law?	Individual and community safety
	1	School and Family	What can citizens do when they disagree with an unfair law?	First Amendment
	2	Neighborhoods	How can someone be a good citizen and break the law?	Boston Tea Party, Susan B. Anthony, Harriet Tubman
	3	Communities Near and Far	How have bad laws in our community been changed?	Expansion of voting rights
	4	State and Region	How was civil disobedience used to end African American enslavement?	The Underground Railroad
	5*	US History	How do citizens in a democracy work to end injustice?	Civil rights movement, Rosa Parks
	6	Beyond the United States	Where and how has civil disobedience been used in places other than the United States? In what ways was civil disobedience effective and ineffective in these other situations?	Mohandas Gandhi (India); Aung San Suu Kyi (Burma/Myanmar); and Nelson Mandela, Steve Biko, and Archbishop Desmond Tutu (South Africa)

*The shaded row indicates the lessons fully developed in Chapter 6 of this book.

Critical Literacy in the Elementary Classroom

While critical literacy is key to CDL (see Chapter 2), it is important to make sure you as a teacher understand the basics of literacy instruction as it applies to critical literacy. For our purposes we are concentrating on using Lewison, Flint, and Sluys's (2002) amalgamation of the vast elements of critical literacy into a usable framework with the following four dimensions for teachers. The following ideas are used throughout the sample unit chapters to illustrate how they can be incorporated into elementary instructional design:

- Disrupting the commonplace
- Interrogating multiple viewpoints
- Focusing on sociopolitical issues
- Taking action and promoting social justice

Lewison, Flint, and Sluys's (2002) work is a thorough overview and we encourage you to read their text; here we paraphrase their main points:

Disrupting the commonplace refers to the importance of students examining content and texts for how they represent others and them as readers.

Interrogating multiple viewpoints centers on understanding various perspectives and analyzing counter narratives to understand who is represented and who is not.

Focusing on sociopolitical issues is concerned with ensuring that students are aware of the larger systems and institutions, and power structures that affect the lives of individuals and communities.

Taking action and promoting social justice emphasizes the need for informed reflection and at times actions that work on behalf of a more just community.

These dimensions were used in the sample lesson chapters as the foundations for student objectives. They are also supported well by the Common Core State Standards for English/Language Arts (CCSS ELA) and the NCSS C3 Framework. Please note that these are broad stances that are a part of the theoretical foundation of critical literacy and should be infused throughout the lessons. Collectively they adhere to the overall purpose of critical literacy, which is to examine literacy, language, and power (Janks, 2010). As a teacher it may help to remember recommendations for teachers posed by Colin Lankshear and Peter McLaren (1993). They advocate that teachers connect learning to students' worlds and experiences, adapt curriculum to maintain a more critical consciousness, and make sure they are informed about subject areas beyond the offerings in the required textbooks.

The role of standards

Throughout this book, we relied on the CCSS ELA and the C3 Framework for Social Studies. The C3 Framework is intended to accompany existing state or district-level social studies standards or to be utilized as a framework to develop new standards (National Council for the Social Studies, 2014, p. 172). Not all states have adopted or implemented these standards so we encourage you to use the standards that are required in your school setting. Two additional sources for national level standards are the National Council for the Social Studies (NCSS) and the International Reading Association (IRA). These standards, available online, are outlined in Table 7.5.

We hope these resources will assist you in thinking about the four guiding civic concepts that are the foundation of CDL. The next chapter includes tools for your specific lesson planning.

TABLE 7.5 NCSS and IRA standards

National Curriculum Standards for Social Studies: A Framework for Teaching, Learning, and Assessment (2010) http://www.socialstudies.org/standards	*International Reading Association Standards for the English Language Arts* http://www.reading.org/General/CurrentResearch/Standards/LanguageArtsStandards.aspx
I. Culture	1. Students read a wide range of print and nonprint texts to build an understanding of texts, of themselves, and of the cultures of the United States and the world; to acquire new information; to respond to the needs and demands of society and the workplace; and for personal fulfillment. Among these texts are fiction and nonfiction, classic, and contemporary works.
II. Time, Continuity, and Change	
III. People, Places, and Environments	2. Students read a wide range of literature from many periods in many genres to build an understanding of the many dimensions (e.g., philosophical, ethical, aesthetic) of human experience.
IV. Individual Development and Identity	3. Students apply a wide range of strategies to comprehend, interpret, evaluate, and appreciate texts. They draw on their prior experience, their interactions with other readers and writers, their knowledge of word meaning and of other texts, their word identification strategies, and their understanding of textual features (e.g., sound-letter correspondence, sentence structure, context, graphics).
V. Individuals, Groups, and Institutions	
	4. Students adjust their use of spoken, written, and visual language (e.g., conventions, style, vocabulary) to communicate effectively with a variety of audiences and for different purposes.

VI.	Power, Authority, and Governance	5.	Students employ a wide range of strategies as they write and use different writing process elements appropriately to communicate with different audiences for a variety of purposes.
VII.	Production, Distribution, and Consumption	6.	Students apply knowledge of language structure, language conventions (e.g., spelling and punctuation), media techniques, figurative language, and genre to create, critique, and discuss print and nonprint texts.
		7.	Students conduct research on issues and interests by generating ideas and questions, and by posing problems. They gather, evaluate, and synthesize data from a variety of sources (e.g., print and nonprint texts, artifacts, people) to communicate their discoveries in ways that suit their purpose and audience.
VIII.	Science, Technology, and Society	8.	Students use a variety of technological and information resources (e.g., libraries, databases, computer networks, video) to gather and synthesize information and to create and communicate knowledge.
IX.	Global Connections	9.	Students develop an understanding of and respect for diversity in language use, patterns, and dialects across cultures, ethnic groups, geographic regions, and social roles.
X.	Civic Ideals and Practices	10.	Students whose first language is not English make use of their first language to develop competency in the English language arts and to develop understanding of content across the curriculum.
		11.	Students participate as knowledgeable, reflective, creative, and critical members of a variety of literacy communities.
		12.	Students use spoken, written, and visual language to accomplish their own purposes (e.g., for learning, enjoyment, persuasion, and the exchange of information).

References

Brophy, J. and Alleman, J. (2008). Early elementary social studies. In L. S. Levstik and C. A. Tyson (Eds.), *Handbook of research in social studies education* (pp. 33–49). New York, NY: Routledge.

Clark, J. S., Vontz, T. S., & Barikmo, K. (2008). Teaching about civil disobedience: Clarifying a recurring theme in the secondary social studies. *Social Studies*, 99(2), 51–56.

Dagger, R. (1997). *Civic virtues: Rights, citizenship, and republican liberalism*. Oxford, UK: Oxford University Press.

Downey, M. & Levstik, L. (1998). Teaching and learning history: The research base. *Social Education*, 52(6), 336–342.

Galston, W. A. (2007). Pluralism and civic virtue. *Social Theory and Practice*, 33(4), 625–635.

Hope, E. C. & Jagers, R. J. (2014). The role of sociopolitical attitudes and civic education in the civic engagement of Black youth. *Journal of Research on Adolescence*, 24(3), 460–470.

Janks, H. (2010). *Literacy and power*. New York, NY: Routledge.

Jefferson, W., Douglas, T., Kahane, G., & Savulescu, J. (2014). Enhancement and civic virtue. *Social Theory and Practice*, 40(3), 499–527.

Kranich, N. (2010). Promoting adult learning through civil discourse in the public library. *New Directions for Adult and Continuing Education*, 127, 15–24.

Lankshear, C. & McLaren, P. L. (1993). *Critical literacy: Politics, praxis, and the postmodern*. Albany, NY: SUNY Press.

Lewison, M., Flint, A. S. & Van Sluys, K. (2002). Taking on critical literacy: The journey of newcomers and novices. *Language Arts*, 79(5), 382–392.

Lindeman, E. C. L. (1935/1987). The place of discussion in the learning process. Reprinted in S. D. Brookfield, *Learning democracy: Eduard Lindeman on adult education and social change*. Kent, UK: Croom Helm.

National Council for the Social Studies. (2014). The C3 framework: One year later. An interview with Kathy Swan. *Social Education*, 78(4), 172–174, 178.

Mazurana, D. E. & Bonds, A. E. (2000). A hostile reception: Women's realities of civil political discourse in democracies. *Peace and Conflict: Journal of Peace Psychology*, 6(4), 325–332.

Pettit, P. (1997). *Republicanism: A theory of freedom and government*. Oxford, UK: Oxford University Press.

Quigley, C. N. & Bahmueller, C. F. (1991). *Civitas: A framework for civic education*. Calabasas, CA: Center for Civic Education.

Rawls, J. (1999). *A theory of justice*. Cambridge, MA: Harvard University Press.

Scheurman, G. (2012). Cold vs. hot war: A model for building conceptual knowledge in history. *Social Education*, 76(1), 32–37.

Smith, W. (2011). Civil disobedience and the public sphere. *The Journal of Political Philosophy*, 19(2), 145–166.

Vesperman, D. P., Bernens-Kinkead, D. J., Loudemilk, L. S., & Neson, G. I. M. (2012). "They mean something more!" Teaching about symbols using balanced integration. *Social Studies and the Young Learner*, 25(1), 10–12.

Wicks, R. H., Wicks, J. L., Morimoto, S. A., Maxwell, A., & Schulte, S. R. (2014). Correlates of political and civic engagement among youth during the 2012 presidential campaign. *American Behavioral Scientist*, 58(5), 622–644.

8
CRITICAL DEMOCRATIC LITERACY
Resources for Application and Implementation

Planning for Critical Democratic Literacy (CDL)-focused social studies and literacy integrated instruction requires understanding content, gathering and evaluating materials, and planning instruction and assessment. This chapter contains several resources to assist you with planning instruction.

Overview of Instructional Strategies for Critical Democratic Literacy

The following strategies, all utilized in this book, have similarities across both social studies and literacy. However, they are different in purpose, even if some of the processes are the same. When integrated, you are asking students to both understand existing information, and to analyze/evaluate in order to construct a new narrative. This is the crux of integration. As a teacher you must understand not only the task but also the content of both disciplines and know how they can be used together effectively to heighten student understandings.

Chronology in Social Studies and Sequencing in Literacy

Chronology is an essential concept in social studies, particularly in history. Chronological thinking is the ability to think about the past, present, and future (National Center for History in the Schools, 1996). The purpose is not to just put events in order, but to consider the historical significance of those events, and to look for patterns and instances of cause and effect across events, as part of historical thinking (Seixas & Morton, 2013). By developing an understanding of chronology, students begin to see how different eras and events are related, as well as to see themselves as part of history. Sequencing in literacy is typically used as a comprehension strategy to assist students in placing events in order. It focuses on literal comprehension of a text (Barton & Sawyer, 2004). Figure 8.1 demonstrates the integration of chronology and sequencing.

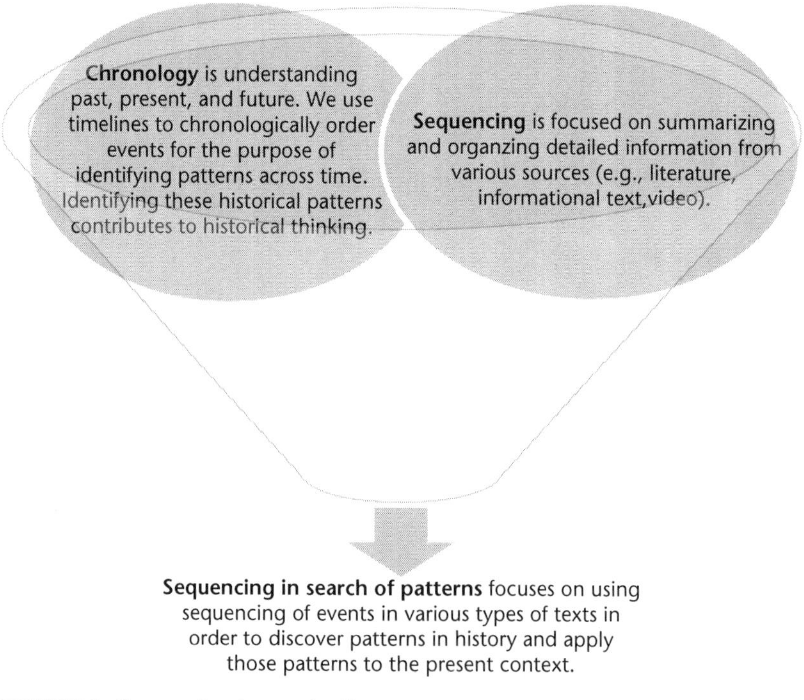

Chronology is understanding past, present, and future. We use timelines to chronologically order events for the purpose of identifying patterns across time. Identifying these historical patterns contributes to historical thinking.

Sequencing is focused on summarizing and organizing detailed information from various sources (e.g., literature, informational text, video).

Sequencing in search of patterns focuses on using sequencing of events in various types of texts in order to discover patterns in history and apply those patterns to the present context.

FIGURE 8.1 Sequencing in search of patterns

Source Analysis in Social Studies and History and Comprehension in Literacy

Primary source analysis, sometimes called historical source work (Barton, 2005; Van Sledright, 2004), is central to the work of historians. The thorough analysis, interpretation, and evaluation of multiple primary sources, as well as secondary sources, are all used to construct new historical narratives. Moving beyond literal comprehension, inferential comprehension requires students to go beyond the text to rely on additional sources of information, such as their prior knowledge about a topic and other texts (Mills, 2010). Figure 8.2 demonstrates the integration of primary source analysis and comprehension as part of CDL.

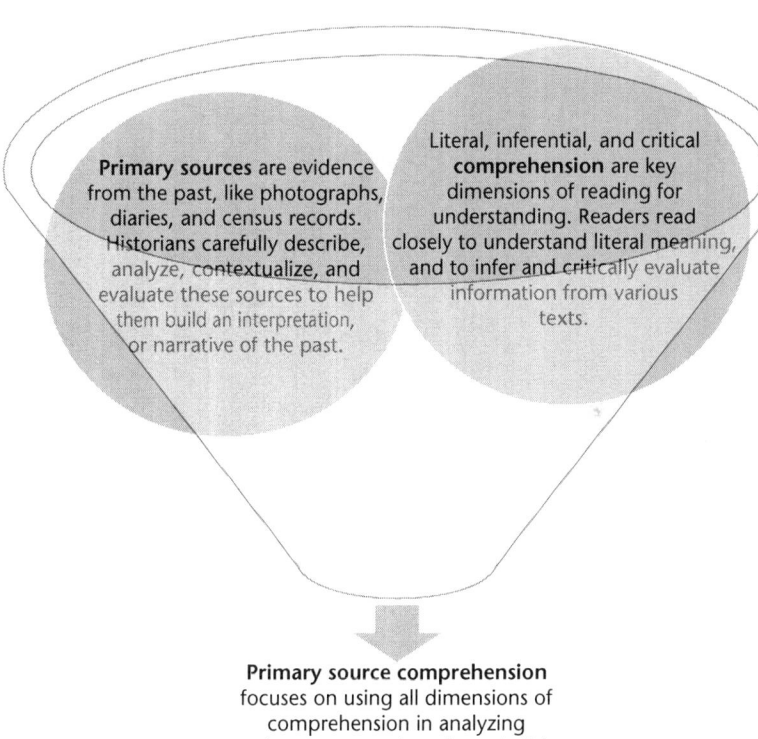

FIGURE 8.2 Primary source comprehension

Inquiry in Social Studies and Informational Text in Literacy

Inquiry in social studies is similar to the scientific inquiry process. However, instead of relying on the testing of physical and biological processes, social studies examines the human condition (e.g., experiences, decisions, events). An inquiry is typically organized around an important question or hypothesis to which there is no obvious or single answer (Obenchain & Morris, 2015). Reading informational text for elementary students brings together comprehension, vocabulary, and writing expository texts skills (Pardo, 2004). Figure 8.3 illustrates the integration of the social studies inquiry process with informational text literacy skills by privileging the disciplinary content and skills.

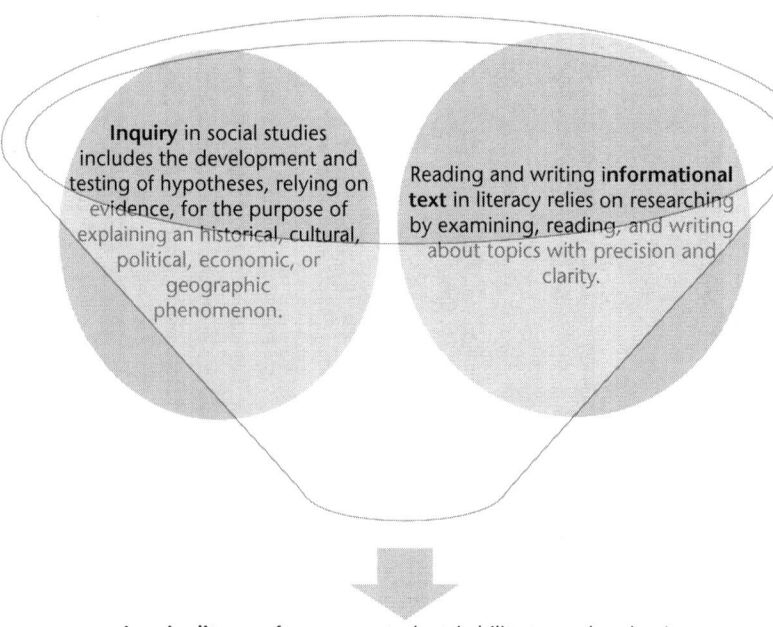

FIGURE 8.3 Inquiry literacy

Critical Democratic Literacy: Resources **147**

Readers' Theater in Social Studies and Literacy

Readers' theater in social studies, particularly history, is used to deepen an understanding of a significant person, era, or event (Obenchain & Morris, 2015). Informational text readings could include reading George Washington's Farewell Address, the Emancipation Proclamation, and a newspaper account of 9/11 witnesses. Readers' theater in social studies could also utilize historical fiction to explore an era or event. Readers' theater in literacy focuses on developing literacy skills such as fluency and comprehension in all types of texts, such as poems and informational texts (Worthy & Prater, 2002). Figure 8.4 illustrates how integrating the social studies and literacy when using readers' theater promotes CDL.

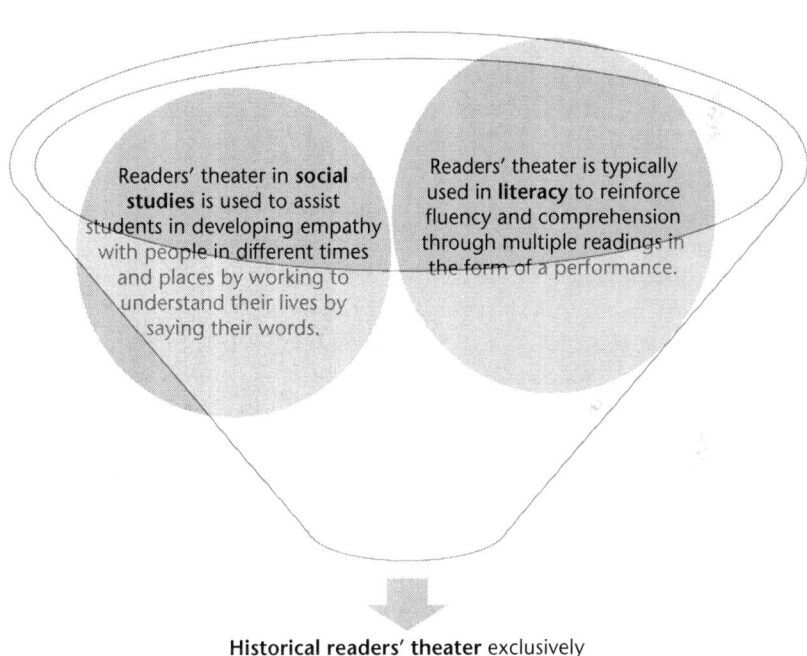

FIGURE 8.4　Historical readers' theater

Teacher Knowledge

In this section, we introduce Lee Shulman's (1986) ideas about teacher knowledge, or the knowledge that every teacher uses in considering what and how to teach. Throughout the book, you have read about the necessity of teachers as educated subjects (Fendler, 1998), the education of citizens, and numerous examples of ways that we, as teachers, and our students become more knowledgeable. In this section, we build on Shulman's categorization of teacher knowledge, focusing on four of those categorizations. We adapt his notions of content knowledge—pedagogical, curricular, and strategic knowledge here—to provide a framework for you to follow as you plan, teach, and assess social studies and literacy. The content knowledge needed by teachers includes understanding both the *what* and the *why* of the discipline. For example, our book includes social studies content about specific individuals including Jane Addams, Malala Yousafzai, Thomas Jefferson, James Madison, and Elizabeth Cady Stanton, among others, as well as eras including the constitutional era and the civil rights movement (CRM). In teaching the CRM, elementary teachers must understand the major events and actors in the US CRM and why the CRM is important for elementary students in relation to civic concepts such as civic virtue, civic engagement, civil discourse, and as Chapter 6 illustrates, civil disobedience. Elementary teachers should also understand that *content knowledge* is also not neutral. Even within the CRM, teachers make choices on what specific content to include. Those decisions affect how critically the era is examined, as well as whether students recognize perennial issues related to racism and social justice. In addition to the content knowledge of each of the disciplines, elementary teachers must also possess *pedagogical content knowledge (PCK)*, which Shulman (1986) explains as the *content knowledge* teachers must understand in a way to teach it, using "the most useful forms of representation . . . the most powerful analogies, illustrations, examples, explanations, and demonstrations—in a word, the ways of representing and formulating the subject that make it comprehensible to others" (p. 9). For the CRM, a teacher must know enough information about the CRM, enough about the discipline of history, as well as how children learn history in order to design appropriate lessons. Knowing the difficulty of connecting children to history because of its chronological distance, a teacher may look to experiences of children from the CRM era. *PCK* also refers to how a teacher understands students' reading levels and how a difficult text would be taught. While children may struggle to connect with the past, they can connect with children of the past. The third form of knowledge, *curricular knowledge*, refers to the programs, instructional materials, and alternatives for teaching that are available to help students learn the content. Finally, we address *strategic knowledge* and adapt it to describe the knowledge teachers need to navigate critical perspectives and the evaluation of themselves, and reflect on their teaching and their students' learning. These ideas are explored in detail in this chapter.

Teacher Knowledge Planning Framework

While these types of knowledge overlap in some areas, it is important to reflect on their distinct parts. This section contains four planning templates with guiding questions based on Shulman's conceptualizations of four types of teacher knowledge and what we, as teachers, need to consider as we plan and reflect on our teaching. We recommend taking time to go through this planning framework as you begin to conceptualize and plan your CDL lessons.

Content Knowledge Planning

Content knowledge reflects the subject area knowledge you need to teach students about the topic. For example, if you are going to teach the CRM you will have some basic knowledge and you may have a few books or curricular materials depending on your grade level, but the first thing you should do is ask yourself the following questions in Table 8.1.

Pedagogical Content Knowledge Planning

PCK is tied to how you should actually teach the content. From our perspective, *PCK* is the most important part of being able to integrate the curriculum for CDL. As a teacher, it is crucial that you understand the civic concepts, as well as the literacy skills of your students, in order for you to create and modify your lessons. For example, some kindergarten teachers may think that teaching civic virtue is too difficult, but it can be done by understanding students' developmental levels and introducing the concept accordingly. In relation to history, one part of an historian's methodology is to utilize primary sources to build an historical narrative. If you are considering using historical photographs, letters, documents, etc., you may want to consider teaching your students how historians work with

TABLE 8.1 Content knowledge planning

What do I already know?	*What do I want to know?*
What do I know about the social studies (civics, economics, geography, history) knowledge?	What more do I need to know to teach the social studies knowledge?
What literacy skills can I address within the lesson?	How can I adapt the text and activities for my students? (ELLs, reading level, background knowledge of students)
What do the standards require?	How can I use the standards together to support social studies and literacy?

TABLE 8.2 Pedagogical content knowledge planning

What do I already know?	What do I want to know?
What do I already know about how to teach the content related to this civic concept?	What more do I need to address the modes/methods of how I want to present the civic concept?
What about this civic concept will be easy and/or difficult for my students and why?	What would be the best way to present the literacy skills? Social studies content and skills?
What analogies, illustrations, examples, explanations, and demonstrations would help present this civic concept?	What would be the best modes for helping students access the literacy skills? Social studies content and skills?

these kinds of documents. This requires thinking through the content while simultaneously thinking about your students. The questions in Table 8.2 can assist you in thinking about your existing knowledge of instructional methods, which methods reflect the academic disciplines you are using, and how you might adapt them for the specific topic.

Curricular Knowledge Planning

Curricular knowledge encompasses all of the materials you have from books, to videos, to standards and assessments. You want to evaluate your curricular materials to determine what can be used, what can be altered, and what you may have to create (see Table 8.3). In the past, you may have been asked to cover curricula using a narrow scope and sequence, often limited to specified materials. We are asking you to go beyond those set curricular materials to better meet the needs of your students.

Strategic Knowledge Planning

Strategic knowledge is a broad notion; for our purposes we adapt it to address the types of situations you may incur as you plan and teach your units. For example, taking a critical perspective can create opportunities for students to be exposed to and evaluate multiple viewpoints. These varied perspectives can raise questions

TABLE 8.3 Curricular knowledge planning

What do I already know?	What do I want to know?
What materials do I currently have available to teach this civic concept?	What additional materials do I need to teach this civic concept?
What criteria will I use to evaluate/justify the materials I will use?	Where can I find additional materials?
How do the materials I have address the variety of learners in my classroom?	How can I modify the materials I have to meet the variety of learners I have?

TABLE 8.4 Strategic knowledge planning

What do I already know?	What do I want to know?
What issues, topics, or concerns may come up in relation to teaching this civic concept?	What is my personal stance toward these issues, topics, or concerns?
How will I handle such issues?	What is my professional stance?

from parents and administrators. In order to effectively engage in critical perspectives you should understand your own thoughts and be prepared to explain the content to others (see Table 8.4). We focus on perspectives that focus on social justice.

Instructional Process Planning Guide

Once you have thought about what you know about your topic; examined your knowledge and resources; determined what else you need to know about the content, concepts, and instructional methods; and referred to your district's standards and assessments, it's time to plan your unit. The process planning guide (Table 8.5) is designed to assist you in laying out your lessons within your unit. The process guide ensures that you have objectives, standards, and your instructional materials coordinated. Early in the planning process, we suggest an initial assessment in order to find out what students already know. That makes it easier to target and choose relevant standards that students need to be introduced to, as well as ones that students have not yet mastered, and to then develop related and measurable learning objectives. We make sure to create another place for assessment at the end of the planning guide, to determine what standards and objectives have been met, as well as to begin the planning cycle all over again for the next series of lessons.

TABLE 8.5 Instructional process planning guide

Civic Concept	
Social Studies	Critical Literacy
⬇	
Initial Assessment	
Students	
Materials	

(Continued)

TABLE 8.5 Instructional process planning guide (*Continued*)

Standards			
NCSS C3 Framework	Literacy Speaking & Listening Standards (CCSS ELA)	Literacy Reading Standards (CCSS ELA)	Literacy Writing Standards (CCSS ELA)
CIVICS HISTORY			

Learning Objectives	
Social Studies	Critical Literacy

Instructional Methods	
Social Studies	Critical Literacy

Reassessment of Students & Materials
Revise and reteach as needed, focusing on standards and objectives
Revisiting the Civic Concept

References

Barton, K. C. (2005). Primary sources in history: Breaking through the myths. *Phi Delta Kappan*, 18(10), 745–753.

Fendler, L. (1998). What is it impossible to think? A genealogy of the educated subject. In T. S. Popkewitz & M. Brennan (Eds.), *Foucault's challenge: Discourse, knowledge, and power in education* (pp. 39–63). New York, NY: Teachers College Press.

Mills, K. A. (2009). Floating on a sea of talk: Reading comprehension through speaking and listening. *The Reading Teacher*, 63(4), 325–329.

Obenchain, K. M. & Morris, R. V. (2015). *50 social studies strategies for K–8 classrooms* (4th ed.). Upper Saddle River, NJ: Pearson.

Pardo, L. S. (2004). What every teacher needs to know about comprehension. *The Reading Teacher*, 58(3), 272–280.

National Center for History in the Schools. (1996). *National standards for history: Basic edition*. Los Angeles, CA: Author.

Seixas, P. & Morton, T. (2013). *The big six historical thinking concepts*. Toronto, Canada: Nelson.

Shulman, L. S. (1986). Those who understand: Knowledge growth in teaching. *Educational Researcher*, 15(2), 4–14.

VanSledright, B. A. (2004). What does it mean to think historically and how do you teach it? *Social Education*, 68, 230–233.

Worthy, J. & Prater, K. (2002). "I thought about it all night": Readers' theater for reading fluency and motivation. *The Reading Teacher*, 56(3), 294–297.

INDEX

Abernathy, R. 112
accountability 8–9
Adams, A. 57, 64, 148
Adams, J. 57
Addams, J. 34–36, 39–54 (*see also* civic virtue); biography of 39, 47; decision-making and 48; as hero 48–51; Hull House and 47; schooling and 47–48
African Americans: civil rights movements 106–7; enslavement of 57–58, 116; suffrage 58; voting rights of 17
amendments 82; *see also* US Constitution
Anthony, S. B. 75
Anti-Federalist Papers 84
Anti-Federalists 82–84, 93
Aristotle 57
Articles of Confederation 83

Bieber, J. 115
Bill of Rights (*see also* civic discourse): of US Constitution 82–84, 93–99, 99t
Bill of Rights: Protecting Our Freedom Then and Now, The 93
biographies 73–74
Blackwell, F. 117
Boston Tea Party 106
Bunting, E. 118
Burns, L. 58
bus incident 106–7, 120–21

CAR; *see* content area reading (CAR)
CCSS; *see* Common Core State Standards (CCSS)
CCSS ELA; *see* Common Core State Standards for English/Language Arts (CCSS ELA)
CDL; *see* Critical Democratic Literacy (CDL)
cell phones 100–101, 100–101t, 103
chronology 78, 144f; historical significance and 71–73; in social studies 144
citizens/citizenship: education on 17–18; engaged 22; multicultural democratic 6; participatory 22; possessing CDL 20; types of 5–6
civic concepts: civic discourse 81–103; civic engagement 56–79; civic virtue 33–54; civil disobedience 105–24
civic discourse 81–103 (*see also* Bill of Rights); background on 81–84; in community 102–3; concept of 24, 81–82, 102–3, 135–36t; Critical Democratic Literacy and 84; deliberation on 102–3; evaluation of 100–102; historical content on 82–84; initial assessment on 86t, 91–92; instructional methods on 89t, 93–100; learning objectives on 89–90t, 92–93, 93t; narrative on 90–103; preparing for lesson on 86–90t, 90; rationale for 84–85; reassessment on 89t, 102; revisiting 90t, 102–3; standards on 86–90t, 92; T-Chart on 91–92, 92t, 96–97, 97t, 103

civic education: barriers to 7–11; in elementary schools 8–9; through literacy 6–7; through social studies 4–6
civic engagement 56–79 (*see also* women's rights movement [WRM]); background on 56–59; in community 78–79; concept of 24, 56–57, 134t; Critical Democratic Literacy and 59; getting involved in 39–40; historical content on 57–59; historical thinking on 67–73; initial assessment on 60–61t, 66; instructional methods for 63t, 71–78; learning objectives on 62–63t, 71, 71t; narrative on 63–79; preparing for lesson on 60–63t, 64–66; rationale for 59–60; reassessment on 63t, 78; revisiting 63t, 78–79; standards on 61–63t, 70; web concept of 74–78
civic republicanism 130
civic virtue 33–54; background on 33–35; in community 53–54; concept of 23–24, 33–34, 131–32t; Critical Democratic Literacy and 35; decision-making and 50–52; development lesson on 45–48; heroes and heroines of 45, 48–50, 49t; historical thinking on 34–35; initial assessment on 37t, 40–44; instructional methods for 39t, 45; learning objectives on 38–39t, 44–45, 45t; narrative on 39–54; post-lesson evaluation on 52–53; preparing for lesson on 37–39t, 39–40; rationale for 35–36; reassessment on 39t, 53; revisiting 39t, 53–54; standards on 37–39t, 44
civil disobedience, 105–24 (*see also* civil rights movement [CRM]); attainment of 119; background on 105–7; in community 123–24; concept of 24, 105–6, 120–21t, 138t; Critical Democratic Literacy and 107; historical content on 106–7; initial assessment on 108–9t, 112–14; instructional methods on 111t, 115–19; learning objectives on 111t, 114–15, 115t; Merriam-Webster definition of 120; narrative on 111–24; post-lesson evaluation of 119–21; preparing for lesson on 108–11t, 112; rationale for 107; reassessment of 111t, 121–23; revisiting 111t, 123–24; standards on 109–11t, 114
civil rights movement (CRM) 105–6 (*see also* civil disobedience); African Americans 106–7; Rosa Parks 106–7; WRM and 106–7
Civil War 45–46, 58
Click, Clack, Moo: Cows That Type 21–22
collective action 119
Common Core State Standards (CCSS) 9–11
Common Core State Standards for English/Language Arts (CCSS ELA) 10, 44–45, 51–52, 70, 77, 92, 114, 139–40
comprehension 145, 145f; primary source 115–19, 145f
concepts: of chronology 78; of democracy 18; development of 54; development strategy of 46; of hero and heroine 45; web 74–78; of Malala Yousafzai 46
concepts of CDL 23–24, 129–41; civic engagement 133–34; civic virtue 130–32; civil discourse 135–36; civil disobedience 137–38
Constitutional Convention 83
content area reading (CAR) 12
content knowledge planning 148, 149t
Cotton, D. 112
criteria 50
critical 17
Critical Democratic Literacy (CDL): citizens possessing 20; critical in 17; critical literacy and 19–20; democratic in 17–19; development of 16; educating for 3–13; in elementary schools 21–24, 139; ideal of 24–25; informed resilient engagement and 16–25; instructional strategies for 143–47; resources for application and implementation of 129–52; standards in, role of 140–41; teaching 33–124; understanding 3–25
critical literacy 19–20, 139
Critical Theory 17
CRM; *see* civil rights movement (CRM)
Cronin, D. 21
culture 7
current standards movements 9–11
curricular knowledge planning 148, 150t

decision-making 48, 50–52
Declaration of Independence 3, 57–58
Declaration of Sentiments 58
deliberation 82, 102–3

democracy: concepts of 18; ideals of 18–19; informed resilient engagement and 16–25; interpretations of 18; public schooling in 17–18
democratic 17–19; *see also* democracy
democratic education 18
development: of CDL 16; strategy of concept 46
Disciplinary Concepts and Tools section of the C3 Framework (NCSS) 44, 70, 92, 114, 139–40
Douglass, F. 58

Edmund Pettus Bridge 122, 122t
education/educating (*see also* civic education): access to 34–35; for CDL 3–13; citizenship 17–18; democratic 18; WRM and 17, 53; Malala Yousafzai and 42, 44, 47–48, 53
elementary schools: CDL in 21–24, 139; civic education in 8–9; literacy in 8–9, 11–13, 139; social studies in 11–13
engaged citizens 22
engagement 75; informed resilient 16–25; political 133
enslavement of African Americans 57–58, 116
equality 18
Equal Rights Amendment 59
evaluative primary source comprehension 118–19

Federalist Papers 84
Federalists 82–84, 93
Founding Fathers 83, 96
Fourteenth Amendment 9
Freedom Rides 112

Gandhi, M. 105–6, 137

Hamilton, A. 83
Haram, B. 35
Henry, P. 83
heroes and heroines 45, 48–51, 49t
Highlander Folk School 106
historical readers' theater 147f
historical significance 71–73
historical source analysis 67–70
history in literacy 145
Hobbes, T. 57
House of Representatives 3–4
Hull House 34, 36, 47

human rights 18
Hunt, J. 58

I Could Do That! Esther Morris Gets Women the Vote 72
ideal of CDL 24–25
If a Bus Could Talk: The Story of Rosa Parks 120
Important Book, The 36, 40–41
informational text 146, 146f
informed resilient engagement 16–25
injustice 53, 107
inquiry 146, 146f
inquiry literacy lesson 97–100, 146, 146f
instructional process planning guide 151–52t
instructional strategies for CDL 143–47; in literacy 143–47; process planning guide and 151–52; in social studies 143–47
International Children's Day 53
International Reading Association (IRA) 10, 140–41t
interpretive primary source comprehension 117–18
IRA; *see* International Reading Association (IRA)

Jay, J. 83
Jefferson, T. 3, 81, 83–84, 93–94, 96, 148
Jim Crow laws 107, 120
justice 18, 45, 112

King, Jr., M. L. 106–7, 112–13, 137
knowledge: content 148, 149t; curricular 148; *pedagogical content (PCK)* 149, 150t; plus 22; strategic 148, 151t; teacher, on teaching CDL 148–51

Lankshear, C. 139
leaders 44–45
Lewis, J. 112
liberty 18
Library of Congress 117
literacy 147f; civic education through 6–7; comprehension in 145; critical 7, 19–20, 139; culture and 7; disciplinary 12; in elementary schools 8–9, 11–13; history in 145; informational text in 146; instructional strategies for CDL in 143–47; readers' theater in 147; sequencing in 144

literal primary source comprehension 117
Locke, J. 57, 81
lunch counter sit-ins 112, 116–17

Madison, J. 83–84, 93–99, 99t, 148
Malala Fund 53–54
Malala Yousafzai: Warrior with Words 42
Manifest Destiny 4
march on Washington 112
Mason, G. 83
McClintock, M. A. 58
McLaren, P. 139
Mexican-American War 105, 137
minimum wage 98–100
Montgomery bus boycott 107, 112
Most Important Thing chart 41–43, 48
Mott, L. 57–58
multicultural democratic citizenship 6

NAACP; *see* National Association for the Advancement of Colored People (NAACP)
National Archives and Records Administration 117
National Association for the Advancement of Colored People (NAACP) 106, 114
National Council for the Social Studies (NCSS) 10, 140–41t; Curriculum Standards 10, 45
National Guard 114
National Woman's Party 58
NCLB; *see* No Child Left Behind (NCLB)
NCSS; *see* National Council for the Social Studies (NCSS)
Nineteenth Amendment 57–59, 64
Nobel Peace Prize 34, 47
No Child Left Behind (NCLB) 8
nonviolence 116, 119–121, 137; *see also* civil disobedience

organized conflict 46

Parks, R. 11, 105, 112–13; biography of 106; bus incident 106–7, 120–21; civil rights movements 106–7; unjust laws 107
participatory citizen 22
Paul, A. 58, 77
PCK; *see* pedagogical content knowledge (PCK)
pedagogical content knowledge (PCK) 149, 150t
Pink and Say 95

planning: content knowledge 148, 149t; curricular knowledge 148, 150t; instructional process for 151–52t; teaching CDL, framework for 149
Pledge of Allegiance 94–95
plus knowledge 22
political engagement 133
political rights 58
Preamble to the US Constitution 3, 94
primary source analysis 67–70, 145f
primary source comprehension 115–19, 145f; evaluative 118–19; interpretive 117–18; literal 117
process planning guide 151–52
property ownership 17
protest laws 106
public schooling 17–18

racial segregation 107
Rawls, J. 18
Revolutionary War 45, 83
Robert's Rules of Order 91
Robinson. J. 112–13
Rousseau, J. J. 57

school/schooling: Jane Addams and 47–48; public, 17–18; segregation in 113–14; Malala Yousafzai and 42, 44, 47–48, 53
Selma to Montgomery March 112, 122, 122t
seminar 82
Seneca Falls Convention 57–58
sequencing 71, 144, 144f
settlement houses 34
Shulman, L. 148
social justice 112
social studies 147f; chronology in 144; civic education through 4–6; in elementary schools 11–13; inquiry in 146; instructional strategies for CDL in 143–47; leaders and 44–45; source analysis in 145
social studies/historical readers' theater (SS/HRT) 94–97, 147
source analysis 145
Spanish American War 45–46
SS/HRT; *see* social studies/historical readers' theater (SS/HRT)
standards: in CDL 140–41; in current movements 9–11
Stanton, E. C. 57–58, 77, 148
Starr, E. 34
Story of Ruby Bridges, The 113

strategic knowledge planning 148, 151t
suffrage 58
Superman 41, 48–51

Taliban 17, 35, 42
T-Chart 91–92, 92t, 96–97, 97t, 103
teacher knowledge on teaching CDL 148–51
teaching CDL 33–124 (*see also* civic discourse, civic engagement, civic virtue, civil disobedience); content knowledge planning for 149; curricular knowledge planning for 150; planning framework for 149; strategic knowledge planning for 150–51; teacher knowledge on 148–51
Terrible Things: An Allegory of the Holocaust 118–19
Thoreau, H. D. 105–6, 137
Three Questions, The 97
Tiananmen Square 115

Ukrainian uprising 115–16, 122–23, 123t
uncivil discourse 91
United Nations 44
United Nations Convention on the Rights of the Child 94
US Constitution 57; Articles of Confederation and 83; Bill of Rights of 82–84, 93–99, 99t; Equal Rights Amendment of 59; Fourteenth Amendment of 9; House of Representatives defined by 3–4; Nineteenth Amendment of 57–59, 64; Preamble to 3, 94
unjust laws 106–7, 114–15

"Votes for Women" 68–69, 69f
voting rights 17, 57–59

war, concept of 45–46
War on Drugs 46
War on Poverty 46
War on Terror 46
web concept 74–78
Westward Expansion 4
White House 58, 79
Wilson, W. 58–59
Women's Day 53
Women's International League for Peace and Freedom 34
Women's Peace Party 34
women's rights movement (WRM) (*see also* civic engagement): civil rights movements and 106–7; education and 17, 53; political rights 58; property ownership and 17; suffrage and 58; through biographies 73–74; voting rights and 57–59
Wonder Woman 48
World War I 46, 58
Wright, M. 58
WRM; *see* women's rights movement (WRM)

Young, I. M. 18
Yousafzai, Malala 33, 35–36, 39–54, 148 (*see also* civic virtue); biography of 39; concept of 46; decision-making and 48, 50–51; education and 42, 44, 47–48, 53; as hero 48–50; injustice and 53; schooling and 42, 44, 47–48, 53; Taliban and 42